D0462727

PERFORMANCE APPRAISAL IN ACADEMIC LIBRARIES
CLIP NOTE #12

Compiled by

Barbara Williams Jenkins, Ph.D.
Dean of Library and Information Services

with the assistance of

Mary L. Smalls, Coordinator
Collection Organization

MILLER F. WHITTAKER LIBRARY
South Carolina State College

College Library Information Packet Committee
College Libraries Section
Association of College and Research Libraries
A Division of the American Library Association

ASSOCIATION OF
COLLEGE
& RESEARCH
LIBRARIES

Published by the Association of College and Research Libraries
A Division of the American Library Association
50 East Huron Street
Chicago, IL 60611-2795
312-280-2515
Toll-free 1-800-545-2433 ext. 2515

ISBN: 0-8389-7444-9

The paper used in this publication meets the minimum requirements of American
National Standard for Information Sciences—Permanence of Paper for Printed
Library Materials, ANSI Z39.48-1984. ∞

Printed in the United States of America.

TABLE OF CONTENTS

SUPPORT STAFF PERFORMANCE APPRAISAL DOCUMENTS

CLIP NOTES COMMITTEE

INTRODUCTION

The College Library Information Packet (CLIP) Notes Program was designed in 1980 by the Continuing Education Committee of the College Libraries Section, Association of College and Research Libraries, a division of the American Library Association. In P. Grady Morein's words,

> the program provides college and small university libraries with state-of-the-art reviews and current documentation on library practices and procedures of relevance to them. The function of the CLIP Notes program is to share information among smaller academic libraries as a means of facilitating decision making and improving performance. The basic premise underlying the program is that libraries throughout the nation are facing numerous challenges due to changing environments and that many of these libraries can benefit by knowing how similar institutions have resolved certain problems.[1]

This *CLIP Note* re-examines the subject of performance appraisal which was surveyed in *CLIP Note #1*, compiled in 1978 and published in 1980. It contained information and documents on practices of the late 1970s.

A survey of the literature showed an increase in the number of articles and surveys on performance appraisal in academic libraries and changes in the treatment of the subject in academic library management books. It is therefore timely that this subject be reviewed to determine practices and trends of the late 1980s.

Purpose

The purpose of this survey was to collect data on current practices regarding performance appraisal in academic libraries for librarians and support staff. Its specific aims were to determine (a) status of performance appraisal; (b) frequency of performance appraisal; (c) type of performance appraisal instrument; (d) uses of the performance appraisal document (i.e., promotion, tenure, salary increments, staff development, retention); and (e) individuals involved in the performance appraisal or review process.

For the purpose of this survey, the definition of performance appraisal was used as it appears in the *ALA Glossary of Library and Information Science*.

> The process of evaluating the performance and behavior of employees individually in their positions for purposes of assessing training needs and determining eligibility for retention, salary adjustments, or promotion. Synonymous with performance evaluation and employee evaluation.

1. P. Grady Morein, "What is a CLIP Note?," *C & RL News* 46,5 (May 1985), 226.

Methodology

The questionnaire was constructed, reviewed by the CLIP Notes Committee, and revised by the author. Two hundred fifty (250) surveys were mailed to academic libraries in September, 1988. These academic libraries represent a universe of colleges and small universities, privately and publicly supported. A follow-up was mailed in December, 1988. In all, 208 surveys or 83% were returned.

FINDINGS

General Characteristics (Questions 1-5)

In regard to FTE (full-time equivalent) number of students, the group of responding institutions had a mean of 1713 and a median of 1408. For FTE faculty, the responding libraries served a mean of 113.3 and a median of 93.

In regard to FTE librarians on the staff, the mean was 6 and the median was 5. The range was from 1 to 19. For support staff, the mean was 8.5 and the median was 6, while the range of FTE support staff was from 1 to 56.

The majority of respondents (58%) indicated that faculty status and rank were held by librarians at their institutions, while 21% indicated that academic status was held but not rank. Thus, in almost four-fifths of the responding libraries, the librarians have academic status.

Performance Appraisal in the Library (Questions 6, 7, and 20)

Most of the responding libraries (88%) have performance appraisal programs. Of those having such programs, 85% include both librarians and support staff in the appraisal process.

Some 25 libraries, 12% of the respondents, had no performance appraisal program (none for librarians and none for support staff). Of these 25, some 17 indicated that their parent institution had decided not to have such a program. For 16 of the 25 libraries with no performance appraisal programs, however, plans exist to install one within the next three years.

Of those libraries which have a performance appraisal program, most indicated that librarians (80%) and staff (91%) are evaluated annually.

The timing for the first performance evaluation of a recently appointed librarian varies considerably, but such an evaluation generally occurs either 3, 6, or 12 months after the person is hired. In contrast, there is more uniformity in the scheduling of a first evaluation for support staff. About 58% of respondents indicated that support staff are evaluated 3 months after being hired, while about 26% reported such evaluation after 6 months.

The variations in the timing of evaluations of librarians may largely be attributable to differences in the academic policies and procedures at various schools, as such policies and procedures apply to librarians in their roles as faculty and/or professional staff. Personnel policies for support staff are typically in line with those for other administrative support staff within the institution.

2

Use of a Performance Appraisal Instrument (Questions 8-9)

There appears to be considerable variation in the origin and development of the performance appraisal instrument used in evaluating librarians. The findings suggest a degree of flexibility as to which instrument may be used in the evaluation of librarians, provided the instrument and approach meet the overall institutional guidelines for evaluation.

In most of the institutions (76%) the support staff are evaluated by the performance appraisal instrument used for college-wide support staff. It is probable that policies for the institution as a whole dictate the practices and procedures for the evaluation of support staff.

Use of Performance Appraisal (Question 10)

The survey results show that the four highest categories of use for librarian evaluations are (1) retention, (2) salary increments, (3) staff development, and (4) promotion.

Using a formal performance appraisal for promotion decisions is more applicable to librarians because most librarians in the responding libraries are located within the academic structure of the institution. Support staff are less likely to be promoted because the levels of staff positions within small and medium-sized libraries are usually limited.

Individual Performance Goals and Objectives (Questions 11-12)

In most of these institutions (77%) the librarians are expected to establish individual performance goals and objectives. In a somewhat smaller percentage (about 52%) the setting of such goals and objectives is expected of support staff.

If the setting of individual goals and objectives is a requirement, whether for librarians or for support staff, then such goals and objectives are generally utilized in the performance appraisal process for that group of employees. The employee can be judged, at least in part, by the progress in achieving the goals and objectives that he or she has set.

Supervisors Evaluating Workers (Questions 13-15)

Most of the responding libraries (86%) have only 1 to 3 librarian supervisors who evaluate other librarians. Not quite so many libraries (61%) have 1 to 3 librarian supervisors who evaluate support staff. In some of the libraries (52%), there are from 1 to 3 staff supervisors who evaluate support staff.

That there are so few supervisors in these libraries is not surprising, since, as noted above, the median number of librarians is 6 and the median number of support staff is 8. In some small libraries the head librarian and perhaps one other librarian may be the only supervisors. In larger libraries, there may be one or more support staff members who serve as supervisors, due to the broader range of functions and larger size of programs and operations.

Performance Appraisal Training Workshops (Questions 16-19)

In only 45 of the institutions (27%) training workshops on conducting performance appraisals are provided for the supervisors of librarians and support staff. Among those institutions that do provide training through workshops, 22% provide annual training. In the other 78%, the training provided is scheduled "as the need arises." Most training workshops of this type are judged to be only "fairly beneficial" to the supervisors in the implementation of the performance appraisal.

Comparison of 1988 Data with 1978 Data

The data from the 1978 *CLIP Note* indicated that most of the college libraries responding to the survey at that time were just beginning to move toward performance appraisal. In contrast, the data from the present survey showed that by 1988, performance appraisal was a standard practice in academic libraries for both librarians and support staff. Another trend apparent in the responding groups was the granting of faculty status and/or rank for all librarians and not just for the library director, as was often the case in 1978.

Summary

Today, the use of performance appraisals for both librarians and members of the support staff is prevalent. Generally, both librarians and support staff are given performance evaluations at least annually. Librarians typically have faculty status and/or rank within the academic structure of the college or university. For librarians, the performance appraisal instrument may either be one that was designed specifically for librarians or one that was patterned after that used for other faculty in the college or university. For support staff, the performance evaluation instrument is usually the same one used for college-wide support staff.

For librarians, performance appraisal is typically used for retention, salary increments, staff development, promotion, and, where applicable, for tenure consideration. For support staff, performance appraisal is typically used for salary increments, retention, and staff development. Use of performance appraisal for decisions about promotion of support staff is not so widespread.

Both librarians and support staff are usually expected to establish individual performance goals and objectives for utilization within the performance appraisal process. Training workshops are not usually made available for supervisors (librarians and support staff) to improve their skills in conducting performance appraisals.

Selection of Performance Appraisal Instruments

A. Forms Used by Libraries for Evaluating Librarians

In selecting librarian forms for inclusion in this *CLIP Note*, the following elements were considered:

- Evaluation sources used: self, patrons, peers, and supervisor/administrator

- Characteristics evaluated: performance, communication, interpersonal skills, professional skills, supervisory abilities, resourcefulness, service to institution, etc.

- Analysis of performance: strengths, weaknesses, recommendations, plans for individual development

- Description of employee's assignments, annual activities, objectives, outcomes, and campus and community involvement

- Description of employee's professional development activities: publications, grants, institutes/workshops, memberships, continuing education, etc.

- Use of short-range and long-range plans for individual/departmental goals and objectives, with timing specified and action statements given.

B. Forms Used by Libraries for Evaluating Support Staff

In selecting support staff forms for inclusion in this *CLIP Note*, the following elements were considered:

- Characteristics evaluated: performance, communication, interpersonal skills, professional skills, supervisory abilities, resourcefulness, service to institution, etc.

- Person's job duties and assignments, annual activities, objectives and outcomes, and general performance

- Analysis of performance: strengths, weaknesses, recommendations, plans for individual development.

This questionnaire is designed to elicit information on performance appraisal in your library and will be kept confidential. For this study, the definition of performance appraisal will be used from the *ALA Glossary of Library and Information Science*--"the process of evaluating the performance and behavior of employees individually in their positions for purposes of assessing training needs and determining eligibility for retention, salary adjustments, or promotion. Synonymous with performance evaluation and employee evaluation." Institutions will not be specifically delineated in analyzing the data.

INSTITUTION AND LIBRARY PROFILE

Institution Name _____ Public _____ Private_____

Address_____

Name of Respondent_____

Title _____

Data for 1988-89:

1. Number of fulltime equivalent students   mean 1713   median 1408

2. Number of fulltime equivalent faculty   mean 113.341   median 93.000

3. Number of fulltime equivalent librarians   mean 6   median 5

4. Number of fulltime equivalent support
   staff in library   mean 8.519   median 6

5. Check the following as it applies to your librarians:

   a. faculty status and rank   _120_

   b. academic status only   _45_

   c. non-academic status   _43_   d. other 15

6. Do you have a performance appraisal program in your library?

   _182_ Yes (if yes, please check the following sub-section where applicable then proceed to question 7).

   a. Librarians and support staff _154_

   b. Librarians performance appraisal program only _10_

   c. Support staff performance appraisal program only _10_

   _25_ No (if no, answer the following sub-section, then proceed to the last page of the questionnaire).

   d. Is it a decision made by the _3_ library, _9_ institution,

   _8_ both, __ other (please specify)_____.

   e. Are there plans to include performance appraisal programs within

   _5_ one year, _8_ two years, _3_ three years.

7. How often is performance appraisal implemented with your staff?

		Librarians	Support Staff
a.	annually__	146	165
b.	every eighteen months__	1	
c.	every two years__	7	
d.	every three years__	5	
e.	other (please specify)_21		

8. Check the following as it applies to your performance appraisal instruments for librarians.

    a. designed for college/university faculty_50_

    b. designed for librarians_51_

    c. combination of the above_30_

    d. other (please specify) __43__ e.g. designed for all professional personnel;__ designed for administrators; narrative report based on college-wide__ instrument for administrative/professional staff.__

9. Check the following as it applies to your performance appraisal instruments for support staff.

    a. designed for college-wide support staff_129_

    b. designed for library support staff_20_

    c. combination of the above_7_

    d. other (please specify) __14__ e.g. designed for non-faculty employees;__ state-wide classified staff.__

10. Is performance appraisal used for: (check where applicable)

		Librarians	Support Staff
a.	Promotion	101	43
b.	Tenure	60	2
c.	Staff Development	103	108
d.	Retention	125	115
e.	Salary Increments	115	123
f.	Other (please specify)	3	

    g. Comments on any of the above, as applied at your institution, that might be useful to academic librarians __30__ e.g. merit with bonus; we are library professionals, not classroom faculty; being considered faculty is more trouble than it's worth; support staff are civil service and I can tell no way in which it is used.__

11. Do staff members establish individual performance goals and objectives?

	Yes	No
a. Librarians	137	40
b. Support Staff	90	82

12. Are these goals and objectives utilized with the performance appraisal process?

	Yes	No
a. Librarians	125	30
b. Support Staff	84	54

13. How many librarian supervisors in your library evaluate librarians? (please check the appropriate category)

    _144_ (1-3)   _17_ (4-6)   _4_ (7-10)   _1_ (11+)

14. How many librarian supervisors in your library evaluate support staff (please check the appropriate category).

    _102_ (1-3)   _45_ (4-6)   _18_ (7-10)   _2_ (11+)

15. How many support staff supervisors in your library evaluate support staff? (please check appropriate category)

    _73_ (1-3)   _8_ (4-6)   _5_ (7-10)   _3_ (11+)

16. Are training workshops held for supervisors (librarians and support staff) to perform performance appraisals _48_ Yes (please proceed to question 17)

    _132_ No (please proceed to question 20).

17. How often are performance appraisal workshops held? (please check appropriate category).

    _10_ annually

    _0_ every two years

    _0_ every three years

    _35_ as the need arises.

18. Are performance appraisal workshops sponsored by: (please circle appropriate category).

    _34_ institution

    _8_ library

    _6_ both

    _2_ other (please specify) _____

19. Have these workshops been beneficial to the supervisors in the implementation of performance appraisal? (please circle the appropriate response)

very	quite	fairly	not too	not at all
2	15	21	3	0

20. Within what time span is the new library staff employee evaluated shortly after being hired?

	Librarians	Support Staff
3 months after being hired	42	112
6 months after being hired	51	49
9 months after being hired	14	3
12 months after being hired	72	28

Please enclose samples of your performance appraisal documents for Librarians and Support Staff. Please check if they can be shared with other academic librarians as examples.

Yes, we can share __

No, we cannot share __

Permission to publish documents:

____ I give permission to publish in a <u>CLIP Notes</u> publication any documents I send with this completed survey.

____ Permission to publish in a <u>CLIP Notes</u> publication any documents I send with this completed survey requires this copyright statement: _____

_____

_____

Thank you for your cooperation with this survey.

A mailing label and self addressed envelope are enclosed for your perusal. Please return survey and documents by <u>NOVEMBER 15, 1988</u> to:

Dr. Barbara Williams Jenkins, Dean
Library and Information Services
Miller F. Whittaker Library
South Carolina State College
Post Office Box 1991
Orangeburg, SC 29117

BWJ/ejc
9/20/88

LIBRARIAN PERFORMANCE
APPRAISAL DOCUMENTS

Dacus Library

FACULTY PERFORMANCE APPRAISAL

IDA JANE DACUS LIBRARY

NAME _____

POSITION AND RANK _____

DATES COVERED BY EVALUATION _____

YEARS OF EXPERIENCE AS A PROFESSIONAL LIBRARIAN _____

PHILOSOPHY AND INTENT

Performance appraisal of all employees in an organization is essential for good personnel management and planning. Without regular and frequent appraisal, an employee cannot place his or her performance in perspective with the expectations of the supervisor or organization. Fulfillment of assigned duties and responsibilities is one of the gauges upon which the employee is rated by his or her supervisor. Other criteria involved in evaluating performance are progress toward completing established goals and objectives and opportunities for future growth.

The function and desired purpose of formal appraisal of librarians at Ida Jane Dacus Library is multi-faceted. As an evaluation tool, it serves the function of allowing the supervisor to look at the work being done by the librarian and communicate how well he or she is performing the duties and responsibilities assigned. In return, it enables the librarian to take a look at himself or herself, by analyzing his or her development and receiving feedback from the supervisor. Other areas in which the appraisal may be used and have an effect are decisions on salary and in the librarian's promotion and tenure process.

It is the primary goal of this appraisal to promote clear and regular communication of professional expectations between librarians and their supervisors. Note should be taken that this is not, nor should it ever serve as, the only form of communication between librarian and supervisor. That it may, in some cases, be the only documented record of interaction is undeniable; however, it should always comprise only a portion of the communication channel which runs throughout every work area.

All librarians at Winthrop College are accorded faculty rank and status, as stated in the school's Faculty Manual. As a result, their appraisal is conducted in a manner which is, in principle and guideline, as similar as possible to that of all other college faculty.

There are three sections covered in the librarian's appraisal:

    Section I   Employee's Self-Evaluation
    Section II   Supervisor's Evaluation
    Section III   Head of Division's and Dean's Evaluation

[The above was composed after perusal of the evaluation forms of numerous libraries. No claim of originality is made.]

13

The completed appraisal form becomes a part of the librarian's permanent record and is kept on file in the office of the Dean. This form, and the rest of the librarian's file, is confidential and should be regarded as such. It is accessible only to:

1. the library faculty member,
2. the supervising librarian,
3. the Dean and Assistant Dean of Library Services,
4. the President of the college,
5. such other administrators of the college as the Dean of Library Services may determine to be in the best interest of the library.

PROCEDURES AND GENERAL INSTRUCTIONS

You will complete this form once a year according to the following timetable. These dates will be supplied by the Dean's office.

BY _____
(First Monday in March)
You will be notified of the forthcoming evaluation process.

BY _____
(First Monday in April)
The self-evaluation has been completed and is ready for your supervisor.

BY _____
(Third Monday in April)
Supervisor reviews the completed evaluation form with you discussing his or her comments.

BY _____
(Third Friday in April)
Head of Division's evaluation has been completed and the completed evaluation form has been submitted to the Dean's office.

BY _____
(Last day in April)
Evaluation form returned from the Dean's Office for your final review and signature. The completed evaluation form has been returned to the Dean's Office to be added to your permanent record.

SECTION I

EMPLOYEE SELF-EVALUATION

List all the responsibilities as specified in your position description. Each position responsibility should be listed regardless of the level of activity. Under each position responsibility there are two parts.

In Part A, explain the ways in which these responsibilities were carried out. Be sure to include major accomplishments that facilitated fulfillment of these responsibilities.

In Part B, list your next year's goals and/or objectives for each responsibility.

For example:

Position Responsibility #1:

Part A   Your comments could include how you have fulfilled this responsibility, problems you have had, exceptional activities, improving performance, etc. Also comment on your previous year's goals and/or objectives and what you did toward accomplishing them.

Part B   Next year's goals and/or objectives for this position responsibility.

Position Responsibility #2:

ETC.

SECTION II

SUPERVISOR'S EVALUATION

1. Comment on employee's job performance. This could include:
    professional knowledge and how the employee implements this
    knowledge; how employee's work complements that of others
    in the library; employee's participation in professional
    development; and suggestions for job development. Consider
    commitment to quality, organization of work, problem
    solving abilities, and supervisory skills. Also consider
    how well the faculty member has met his/her goals/objec-
    tives.

2. Comment on employee's individual attributes. Consideration
    could be made of: interaction with others on the job; oral
    and written communication skills; openness to new ideas;
    flexibility; cooperation; initiative; and judgement.

17

SECTION III

HEAD OF DIVISION'S EVALUATION

COMMENTS ON OVERALL EMPLOYEE PERFORMANCE:

DEAN'S EVALUATION

COMMENTS ON OVERALL EMPLOYEE PERFORMANCE:

Winthrop College

SIGNATURE PAGE

DATE _____

(Signature of Dean)

DATE _____

(Signature of Supervisor)

DATE _____

(Signature of Division Head)

I acknowledge that I have seen the entire Librarian Performance Appraisal. My acknowledgement of this does not indicate agreement or disagreement with the evaluation contained in this report.

DATE _____

(Signature of Library Faculty Member)

Winthrop College

OVERALL RATING TO BE ASSIGNED BY DEAN

Name _____   Position Title _____

Unit or Dept. _____   Date _____

____ **Outstanding** - Truly exceptional performance attained
by no more than an exceptionally small number of
faculty.

____ **Exceeds Requirements** - Performance that surpasses what
is generally expected of faculty a majority of the
time.

____ **Meets Requirements** - Competent day-to-day performance
is attained. Any shortcomings are generally balanced
by some superior performance characteristics. This
level of performance is generally attained by the
majority of faculty.

____ **Needs Improvement** - Day-to-day performance shows some
limitations that are not balanced by any superior
performance characteristics. This level of performance is demonstrated by only a small number of
faculty and deficiencies must be corrected before the
next appraisal.

____ **Unsatisfactory** - Day-to-day performance shows
significant limitations and definite need for improvement is noted. This level of performance is rarely
demonstrated. Improvement is essential to continued
employment.

MARY WASHINGTON COLLEGE
PROFESSIONAL LIBRARIAN PEER EVALUATION

Evaluation of _____   Date covered _____

Each professional librarian is asked to evaluate frankly and objectively each factor (one is low, with nine the highest rating) "N" stands for no basis of judgement. Use the reverse side for additional comments. Evaluation forms will remain confidential under all circumstances.

Evaluation by _____   On the basis of my evaluation, I do ___ I do not ___ recommend merit pay.

Factor	Remarks	Rating
Adaptability (ability to adjust to changing circumstances)		1 2 3 4 5 6 7 8 9 N
Attitude (acceptance of criticism; tact; acceptance of suggestions; civility)		1 2 3 4 5 6 7 8 9 N
Interest and participation in College community		1 2 3 4 5 6 7 8 9 N
Professional effectiveness (knowledge of job; awareness of Library developments)		1 2 3 4 5 6 7 8 9 N
Professional relationship with colleagues (cooperativeness; willingness to suggest improvements; positive concern for Library programs)		1 2 3 4 5 6 7 8 9 N
Relations with library public (approach-ability; responsiveness)		1 2 3 4 5 6 7 8 9 N

21

MARY WASHINGTON COLLEGE
LIBRARY DIRECTOR'S ANNUAL EVALUATION OF LIBRARY FACULTY

Name _____ Period Covered _____

Position _____

Qualities	Outstanding/ Excellent	Above Average	Average/ Satisfactory	Improvement Needed	Unsatisfactory	Not Applicable
A. PERSONAL ATTRIBUTES						
Initiative						
Stability						
Adaptability						
Judgement						
Sense of Responsibility						
B. PROFESSIONAL QUALITIES						
Professional competence						
Professional activities						
Professional ethics						
Relations with Library public						
Awareness of academic community and current affairs						
C. JOB PERFORMANCE						
Attitude						
Organization of work						
Quality of work						
Quantity of work						
Planning and decision-making						
Acceptance and use of criticism						
Supervisory skills						
Supervisory relations						

COMMENTS

Signature of Librarian _____ Date _____

I agree with this evaluation _____ I do not agree with this evaluation _____
  (Explanation of disagreement may be submitted in writing in within 48 hours. When submit
  the explanation should be forwarded as part of the evaluation.)

Signature of Professional Librarian _____

Position _____ Date _____

Original filed in personnel ofc.; copy 1 in Library Director's ofc.; copy 2 to employee

MARY WASHINGTON COLLEGE

KEY TO LIBRARY DIRECTOR'S ANNUAL EVALUATION OF LIBRARY FACULTY

A. Personal Attributes

Qualities	Outstanding/Excellent	Above Average	Average/Satisfactory	Improvement Needed	Unsatisfactory	Not Applicable
Initiative	Exceptionally creative; shows great initiative; keenly appreciative of possibilities for improvement in operations and acts accordingly, within allowable limits.		Resourceful to a limited extent; performs obvious tasks unasked; sometimes offers suggestions and sees possibilities for improvement of operations.		Needs direction; almost never acts without being told to do so; seldom expresses an opinion; even when asked.	
Stability	Even-tempered, tactful and courteous, even under pressure; self-controlled in any situation.		Usually pleasant; self-controlled and courteous under ordinary circumstances.		Irritable; unpredictable or otherwise unpleasant; arouses antagonism; on occasion inconsiderate; easily upset or angered.	
Adaptability	Exceptionally open-minded; eager to consider the ideas of others; willing to subordinate own ideas to group needs; not upset by changes deemed necessary; willing to pursue goals by alternative means.		Moderate acceptance of change; usually willing to accept new ideas; able to work within a prescribed situation.		Usually rejects new methods; resents change; sees only one side of a question; own work patterns of more importance than group needs.	

23

A. Personal Attributes (continued)

Qualities	Outstanding/Excellent	Above Average	Average/Satisfactory	Improvement Needed	Unsatisfactory	Not Applicable
Judgement	Sees the important aspects of problems; makes sound decisions readily; learns from errors.		Usually makes tenable decisions; not always aware of probable results of decisions; judgement generally good.		Indecisive; poor judgement.	
Sense of Responsibility	Accepts responsibility readily; recognizes and respects lines of authority; always punctual; exercises great care in meeting schedules and deadlines.		Usually accepts responsibility and recognizes lines of authority; is usually careful in meeting schedules and deadlines; usually punctual.		Accepts responsibility poorly; ignores lines of authority; unable to recognize organizational relationships; careless about punctuality.	

B. Professional Qualities

Qualities	Outstanding/Excellent	Above Average	Average/Satisfactory	Improvement Needed	Unsatisfactory	Not Applicable
Professional Competence	Highly knowledgeable in professional areas of expertise; constantly learning on the job; develops own capabilities continually.		Adequate knowledge of own job and subject area; some continuing effort made to increase knowledge		Lacks competence in professional knowledge; makes little effort to improve.	
Professional Activities	Holds committee position or office in one or more professional organizations; keeps well abreast of literature and new developments in the profession.		Moderate participation in professional groups; adequate familiarity with literature and new developments in the profession.		No interest beyond own job; rarely or never attends professional meetings; not aware of new developments in the profession.	

24

B. Professional Qualities (continued)

Qualities	Outstanding/Excellent	Above Average	Average/Satisfactory	Improve- ment Needed	Unsatisfactory	Not Appli- cable
Profes- sional ethics	Maintains exemplary standard of professional conduct; always represents the Library and colleagues in the best light.		Usually maintains profes- sional standards of conduct; usually represents the Library and colleagues in the best light.		Disloyal to library policies and procedures; makes no effort to convey a profes- sional attitude to patrons; lacks discretion.	
Relations with Library public 25	Enthusiastic; easily ap- proached and responsive; offers help readily; exerts great effort to understand the patron's needs and to assist him.		May not offer help but gives it willingly on request; usually pleasant; makes some effort to understand the patron's needs and to assist him.		Appears unapproachable; indifference apparent to patron; makes little or no effort to understand patron.	
Awareness of academic community and current affairs	Keen aware of cultural and current affairs; able to relate these needs to the academic community; often anticipates needs of stu- dents and professors; actively participates in college functions.		Average awareness of campus affairs and ability to apply these needs to academic community; occasionally acts in anticipation of needs; generally participates in college activities.		Little or no effort made to keep abreast of current, cultural, or community affairs; seems unaware of any relationship between these affairs and library functions.	

C. Job Performance

Qualities	Outstanding/Excellent	Above Average	Average/Satisfactory	Improvement Needed	Unsatisfactory	Not Applicable
Attitude	Enthusiastic; eager to improve quality of work or service; ability to disagree with supervisor and still willing to carry out assigned responsibilities; engenders a feeling of esprit de corps.		Exerts some effort to improve self and quality of work; generally accepts direction; works acceptably as a team member.		Indifferent; makes little or no effort to improve quality of work; resents supervision.	
Organization of work	Analyzes and organizes work readily; sees relationship to other tasks; sets sound priorities.		Organizes work satisfactorily; accomplishes tasks reasonably and in balance with other tasks to be performed.		Work lacks proper planning; very close supervision is required.	
Quality of work	Exceptionally accurate and complete; accomplishes tasks fully and correctly; results always dependable.		Generally accurate and complete; results usually dependable.		Many errors; work must usually be checked and often redone; leaves task uncompleted.	
Quantity of work	Accomplishes an excellent amount of work; makes best use of time; exerts great effort in an intelligent manner with effective results; time spent on problems proportional to their importance; always completes tasks on time.		Accomplishes assigned tasks; sometimes volunteers; time spent sometimes not in proportion to importance of tasks; usually completes tasks on schedule.		Unacceptable; lacks industry; unable to distinguish between unimportant and important tasks; ineffectual use of time.	

26

C. Job Performance (continued)

Qualities	Outstanding/Excellent	Above Average	Average/Satisfactory	Improvement Needed	Unsatisfactory	Not Applicable
Planning and decision-making	Sees possibilities; makes sound plans for carrying out operations; organizes resources well; grasps total situation.		Usually organizes well; generally grasps total situation.		Indecisive; cannot plan operations; misjudges amount of time or resources needed; does not grasp total situation.	
Acceptance and use of criticism 27	Always accepts direction and criticism without personal pique; uses criticism as a means for improvement; welcomes opinions of others.		Generally accepts direction and criticism and makes effort to use it.		Resents criticism; unwilling to consider suggestions for improvement of work.	
Supervisory skills	Excellent ability to give clear instructions and carry out supervisory duties thoroughly; aware of overall situation and attentive to details. Inspires confidence in leadership ability.		Adequate instruction and supervision given staff; sometimes incomplete knowledge of necessary details; occasionally not sufficiently aware of overall situation.		Inflexible; instructions inadequate or vague; supervision uncertain or sporadic; no attempt made to train; no knowledge of necessary details.	
Supervisory relations	Outstanding judgement and fairness in allocating tasks; makes great effort to support supervisor as well as those supervised fairly; sets and encourages high standards; easily approached; is outstanding in motivating subordinates.		Judgement usually unbiased; sets generally satisfactory performance standards; usually consistent in assigning tasks fairly to employees; generally sensitive to interpersonal relationships.		Poor judgement of capabilities of workers; fails to support fairly supervisor or those supervised; ignores needs of employees.	

LIBRARY FACULTY SELF-EVALUATION AND
ANNUAL ACTIVITIES REPORT

Name _____   Date _____

Department _____   Signature _____

Please complete and submit this form to your department chairperson by the
announced deadline. Include a second copy for the Dean's Office, and also two
copies of your current vita.

I.   Responsibilities

Set forth what you see as your principle responsibilities to the
College. To what extent are the things the College actually asks of you
the things you think it ought to ask of you? Are your particular
talents and interests and professional priorities being appropriately
recognized, used and supported by the College?

II. Professional Initiatives and Plans

What are your personal professional goals and objectives? In what areas of professional activity do you anticipate taking your primary personal initiatives over the next five years? What sorts of opportunities for professional development would be most useful to you? What would you seek to make of those opportunities? How do those plans fit in with the mission of the College, as you understand it?

III. Retrospective

What are the principal components and directions of your professional activities over the past five years? (Note in particular any significant changes in direction or in emphasis. Comment upon what you consider to be noteworthy accomplishments and professional satisfactions over the period. If you wish, comment also upon disappointments, setbacks and frustrations, especially if you see correctable College shortcomings as responsible for them.

IV. <u>Activities over the Calendar Year, 1985</u>.

    1.   Describe any specific accomplishments or special projects completed, above and beyond the regular schedule of work.

_____

_____

_____

_____

_____

    2.   List committee assignments (college or departmental), clubs advised, organizations sponsored or other activity of service to the College.

_____

_____

_____

_____

    3.   (a)   List membership in professional organizations and meetings attended.

_____

_____

_____

_____

           (b)   List offices, committee assignments, programs planned for professional organizations.

_____

_____

_____

_____

(c)   List other information in the area of professional development
such as articles published, papers presented, grants applied
for or received, institutes or workshops attended, <u>etc</u>.

_____

_____

_____

_____

4.   List other pertinent information.

_____

_____

_____

_____

5.   Summary statement.

_____

_____

_____

_____

PENNSTATE

STAFF EXEMPT AND STAFF NONEXEMPT EMPLOYEE PERFORMANCE APPRAISAL

Objectives

The staff performance appraisal system is designed to enhance:

1. COUNSELING AND COMMUNICATION. An employee should be evaluated on his/her performance on a regular basis; work related issues of mutual concern to the employee and the supervisor should be discussed, and efforts to establish performance goal should be initiated.

2. PROFESSIONAL DEVELOPMENT. The evaluation process should be used to identify individual professional development need and opportunities, consistent with the professional goals of the employee and the advanced training skills appropriate for the job an office.

3. PERSONNEL DECISIONS. Performance appraisals can contribute to a variety of personnel actions, including among others, con siderations for promotions and salary increases.

NOTE: Some employees have been called upon or have volunteered to participate in University affirmative action activities. These ac tivities are frequently in addition to an employee's regular job. Any involvement in such activities should be considered alon with the employee's regular work performance when completing an appraisal. While it is important for each employee to per form all of his or her regular duties well, performance appraisals should take into account the employee's entire contribution t the University.

Instructions

The first eight PERFORMANCE CRITERIA may be utilized for all Staff Exempt and Staff Nonexempt employees. The ninth criteric (Supervisory Ability) should be utilized only for employees with supervisory responsibilities.

For each PERFORMANCE CRITERION (sections A through I), the appraiser must:

(1) Provide a performance rating by circling the appropriate number (1 to 12), or
(2) Write a narrative appraisal in the "Supporting Comments" section, or
(3) Provide both a rating and a narrative in the "Supporting Comments."

For the OVERALL EVALUATION (section J), the appraiser MUST provide a numerical performance rating (1 to 12).

Appraisers are reminded of the added value of the narrative sections and are encouraged to supplement the rating with supporting con ments and, where appropriate, suggestions. For each PERFORMANCE CRITERION on which the employee is given an inadequa rating (i.e., 1 to 3), the appraiser MUST provide supporting comments.

In any case where performance under a specific criterion or the OVERALL EVALUATION of an employee is considered to be inade quate, the "Suggestion" portion of the form should also be used. It may be helpful if suggestions, such as recommendations for trai ing or the development of performance objectives, are discussed and jointly agreed upon between the supervisor and the employee

Some of the PERFORMANCE CRITERIA may not be appropriate to a particular position. In such circumstances, simply indica "Not Applicable" under the narrative for the criterion. You may attach a separate piece of paper listing any other criteria which a more applicable to the employee's position, utilizing the same evaluation procedures outlined above.

The descriptive phrases under each PERFORMANCE CRITERION are intended only as suggestions of attributes to be considered. I particular phrase or behavioral example appears to be inappropriate in appraising an employee, the supervisor may simply cross th phrase out. Further clarification of any evaluation may, of course, be added in the "Supporting Comments" section.

Blank copies of the appraisal form may be made available to employees at any time. Furthermore, a mutual review of the employee position description either during or prior to the interview is encouraged to insure the currency and accuracy of the position descriptio as well as establish a basis for understanding the duties being appraised.

STAFF EXEMPT AND STAFF NONEXEMPT EMPLOYEE PERFORMANCE APPRAISAL

EMPLOYEE NAME: _____ POSITION TITLE: _____

COLLEGE/DEPT.: _____ PERIOD COVERED: FROM _____ TO _____

DATE STARTED AT UNIVERSITY: _____ DATE STARTED THIS POSITION: _____

PERFORMANCE CRITERIA

A. JOB KNOWLEDGE: The demonstration of technical, administrative, managerial, supervisory or other specialized knowledge required to perform the job. Consider degree of job knowledge relative to length of time in the current position. If applicable, consider the individual's endeavors to increase job knowledge through additional formal or informal study, seminars, readings, and other professional activities both on and off the job.

1	2	3	Displays deficiencies in job knowledge; further training required.
4	5	6	Shows strength sometimes but is not consistent.
7	8	9	Demonstrates average to high level of job knowledge.
10	11	12	Demonstrates consistently high level of job knowledge.

Supporting Comments: _____

Suggestions: _____

B. PLANNING AND ORGANIZATIONAL EFFECTIVENESS: The extent to which the employee effectively plans, organizes, and implements tasks or programs. Consider the extent to which the employee's performance displays the basic fundamentals of good organization and work planning and the employee's effectiveness in time management. Consider the degree to which the employee meets deadlines, handles emergencies, and appropriately establishes goals and priorities. Assess the individual's productivity compared to the standards of the position.

1	2	3	Displays poor planning; lack of organization apparent even in routine assignments; frequently misses deadlines.
4	5	6	Does routine tasks adequately; difficulty in managing multiple or complex assignments; occasionally misses deadlines.
7	8	9	Average or better; most tasks are planned, organized, and implemented effectively and on time.
10	11	12	Displays outstanding ability to plan, organize, and implement tasks and programs and to meet deadlines.

Supporting Comments: _____

Suggestions: _____

C. INTERPERSONAL RELATIONS: How well the employee gets along with other individuals in the performance of job duties. Consider effectiveness of relations with co-workers, subordinates, supervisor and, if applicable, the general University community and the public in the handling of position responsibilities. Consider the employee's cooperativeness, tact and courtesy.

1	2	3	Has difficulty in relating to others; not readily cooperative.
4	5	6	Relates to others fairly well; works better with some persons than others.
7	8	9	Works well with others; facilitates cooperation.
10	11	12	Is very effective interpersonally; works extremely well with subordinates, peers, and superiors.

Supporting Comments: _____

Suggestions: _____

D. ATTITUDE: Enthusiasm, dedication and interest displayed regarding position responsibilities and duties. Consider whether the employee expresses willingness to undertake projects, supports organizational goals and endeavors, and demonstrates flexibility in response to changing circumstances.

1 2 3 Generally displays negative attitude toward job; criticizes without offering constructive suggestions; inflexible.

4 5 6 Accepts job duties, occasionally with reluctance.

7 8 9 Displays interest in duties and responsibilities; flexible in response to changing circumstances.

10 11 12 Highly dedicated and enthusiastic; strongly supportive of organizational goals.

Supporting Comments: _____

Suggestions: _____

E. INITIATIVE: The degree to which the employee is self-starting and assumes responsibilities when specific directions are lacking. Consider how well the employee follows through on assignments, taking appropriate independent action when necessary, and the relative amount of supervision required.

1 2 3 Needs detailed instructions; requires constant supervision to keep assignments going.

4 5 6 Follows through on some assignments without continuous direction; requires some follow-up to keep assignments progressing.

7 8 9 A self-starter; follows through on assignments independently.

10 11 12 Exceptionally self-reliant; completely follows through on assignments.

Supporting Comments: _____

Suggestions: _____

F. RESOURCEFULNESS: Extent to which employee devises ways and means to deal with challenges in the performance of job duties. Consider the modification of, or recommendations for the modification of, existing methods or procedures to meet new or changing circumstances and the development of new ideas or methods.

1 2 3 Rarely develops more effective ways of handling assignments.

4 5 6 Occasionally offers worthwhile ideas and suggestions when encouraged to do so.

7 8 9 Has necessary resourcefulness to devise or suggest new methods, or to modify existing ones, to meet changing circumstances.

10 11 12 Frequently makes worthwhile suggestions; readily develops ideas and solutions to problems.

Supporting Comments: _____

Suggestions: _____

G. JUDGMENT: Evidence of ability to analyze available data or circumstances concerning a situation, develop alternative solutions and recommend or select a proper course of action.

1 2 3 Makes frequent errors in judgment; often overlooks consequences of decisions.

4 5 6 Judgment usually sound under normal circumstances; occasionally exercises questionable judgment.

7 8 9 Exercises good judgment; aware of impact of decisions on related areas.

10 11 12 Exceptionally sound and sensible judgment; foresees and evaluates impact of decisions on related areas.

Supporting Comments: _____

Suggestions: _____

COMMUNICATION SKILLS: Effectiveness in conveying ideas, information and directions to others. Consider clarity of oral and written communications as related to the employee's responsibilities.

2   3   Displays an inability to communicate clearly.

5   6   Sometimes lacks clarity or conciseness; generally can communicate desired information.

8   9   Communicates in an organized, clear and concise manner.

11   12   An outstanding communicator; can communicate complex information extremely well.

pporting Comments: _____

ggestions: _____

SUPERVISORY ABILITY: COMPLETE ONLY FOR INDIVIDUALS WITH SUPERVISORY RESPONSIBILITY. Extent to which the employee applies sound, acceptable supervisory practices in the execution of his/her supervisory responsibilities. Consider evidence of demonstrated skill in arousing interest and enthusiasm in subordinates rather than solely relying on authority to get the job done. Consider the employee's effectiveness in selecting and developing personnel.

2   3   Causes morale problems; does not adequately handle employee relations.

5   6   Somewhat competent as supervisor but is not consistent.

8   9   Encourages subordinates in self-development; creates and maintains a comfortable, cooperative work environment.

11   12   Dynamically leads subordinates to discover their own potential within their positions; provides inspiration and outstanding leadership to subordinates.

pporting Comments: _____

ggestions: _____

OVERALL EVALUATION: The overall evaluation should reflect the assessment of the employee's total performance, based upon the foregoing criteria. In making the assessment, consider the criteria according to the employee's duties and responsibilities, taking care not to overemphasize one particular criterion.

2   3   Improvement is required in order to perform at an acceptable level.

5   6   Generally performs adequately; need for improvement in specific areas is evident.

8   9   Performs duties and responsibilities well; occasionally excels.

11   12   A noteworthy employee; this employee is a top performer.

pporting Comments: _____

ggestions: _____

_____   _____
gnature of the Appraiser   Date

_____   _____
oncurrence of Administrative Officer   Date

_____   _____
Signature of Individual Appraised   Date

Signature indicates only that the evaluation has been reviewed, and does not necessarily signify concurrence. A response to this appraisal may be made on a separate sheet and attached.

THE PENNSYLVANIA STATE UNIVERSITY AT HARRISBURG
THE CAPITAL COLLEGE
MIDDLETOWN, PENNSYLVANIA 17057

ANNUAL FACULTY ACTIVITY REPORT, ACADEMIC YEAR 19___ - 19___
(For campus use only)

Name _____

Rank and Title _____

Division and Program _____

Date of initial appointment to the University _____

Current Appointment: Standing, A Plan__; Standing, M Plan__; Fixed Term, Type I__

Graduate Faculty Status: Nonmember___; Associate member___; Senior member ___

I. Teaching*

   A. Summary of Courses Taught, Summer through Spring.

Term	Abbreviation and Number	Title	Credits	Final Enrollment
____	_____	_____	___	____
____	_____	_____	___	____
____	_____	_____	___	____
____	_____	_____	___	____
____	_____	_____	___	____
____	_____	_____	___	____
____	_____	_____	___	____
____	_____	_____	___	____

   B. Advising Responsibilities

	Number of Students	
	Undergraduate	Graduate
Summer Session	_____	_____
Fall Semester	_____	_____
Spring Semester	_____	_____

Note: Continue entries on separate sheets as necessary.

36

II. Research

    A.   Publications (use bibliographic form including page numbers; include articles
        accepted for publication; indicate if journal is refereed):

    B.   Manuscripts in progress (indicate actual or anticipated date of submission):

    C.   Research Projects, grants and contracts (date, title, submitted to, amount):

37

D. Graduate papers and theses supervised:

Student	Program	Semester Begun	Semester (to be) Completed
_____	_____	_____	_____
_____	_____	_____	_____
_____	_____	_____	_____
_____	_____	_____	_____
_____	_____	_____	_____
_____	_____	_____	_____

E. Membership on graduate degree candidates' committees (except as first reader):

	Number
Summer	_____
Fall	_____
Spring	_____

F. Creative accomplishments (sculptures, paintings, musical compositions, films, novels, poems, etc.):

G. Other evidences of research accomplishment (identify patents, new product development, etc.):

III. Scholarship and Mastery of Subject Matter

   A. Pursuit of advanced degrees, further academic study:

B. Participation in seminars and workshops (short description of activity, with titles, dates, sponsor, etc.):

C. Papers presented at technical and professional meetings (meeting and paper titles, listed chronologically in bibliographic form):

D. Speaking engagements or other activities in which there was significant use of expertise (consulting, services to government agencies, professional and industrial associations, educational institutions, etc.):

E. New courses developed:

F.   New methods of teaching established courses:

G.   Honors or awards for scholarship or professional activity:

H.   Membership and active participation in professional and learned societies
     (indicate offices held, committee work, other responsibilities):

IV. Service to the University and the Public

A.   Service to the University

1.   Committee work on Division, Campus and University levels (indicate
     offices held):

2. Participation in campus and/or University-wide governance bodies and related activities:

3. Administrative support work (college representative, etc.):

B. Service to the Public

1. Participation in community affairs as a representative of the University:

2. Service to governmental agencies at federal, state and local levels:

3. Service to industry:

4. Service to public and private organizations

_____   _____
Signature   Date

Form revised 3-8-84

Georgia College
EVALUATION OF LIBRARY FACULTY (PILOT STUDY, 1986 rev,)

PROCEDURES

The following steps are to be followed in completing the evaluation forms:

1. The library faculty member will review his/her job description, rate himself/herself according to the established criteria in each major area of responsibility by checking the appropriate box, and make any necessary revisions to reflect changes in the listed duties.

2. The supervisor will review the faculty member's job description, rate the faculty member in each major area of responsibility with the exception of the last category, and make any necessary revisions to reflect changes in the listed duties. The supervisor will complete Professional Performance Evaluation and submit it to the Director of Libraries.

3. The library faculty, after completing Step 1, receives the supervisor's evaluation form to review.

4. The library faculty and supervisor discuss their respective responses. This is a most important step in the process and careful and sensitive attention should be given to it. If responses are at variance and agreement cannot be reached, comments may be attached in writing.

5. The library faculty and supervisor jointly complete summary.

6. The Director of Libraries completes the Summative Evaluation Form for each faculty member based on input from supervisor's ratings and recommendations, personal observation, and the individual faculty report.

7. The Director of Libraries reviews and signs the form, making any appropriate oral or written comments.

This Performance Evaluation Form is designed to accomplish the following objectives.

1. Annually update the library faculty's job description.

2. Provide a clearer understanding of the position.

3. Evaluate work performance.

4. Enhance communication between library faculty and supervisor.

7.02   EVALUATION DEFINITIONS

In an effort to provide for consistency of evaluation, the following definitions might provide guidance.

Noteworthy: Truly exceptional performance generally attained by no more than a small number of an organization's employees.

Good: Superior performance that surpasses what is generally expected of employees a majority of the time.

Satisfactory: Competent   day-to-day   performance   is   attained.   Any shortcomings   are   generally   balanced   by   some   superior   performance characteristics. This level of performance is generally attained by the majority of an organization's employees.

Needs Improvement: Day-to-day performance generally shows some limitations that are not balanced by any superior performance characteristics. This level of performance needs counseling and is generally demonstrated by only a small number of an organization's employees.

Unsatisfactory: Day-to-day performance shows significant limitations and a definite need for improvement. This level of performance is generally demonstrated by no more than an exceptionally small number of an organization's employees.

43

SAMPLE

JOB TITLE: Coordinator of Media Services

REPORTS TO: Director of Libraries

1. Supervise all production work.

   U NI S G N

2. Determine and make recommendations for Media Services budgetary needs; set priorities for budgetary expenditures; prepare appropriate request forms.

   U NI S G N

3. Coordinate all aspects of G.C. television.

   U NI S G N

4. Supervise, schedule, train, and evaluate media staff and make recommendations to the Director regarding personnel in the area.

   U NI S G N

5. Plan, implement, supervise, and evaluate the system for inventory, scheduling, delivering, and repairing of all equipment and materials.

   U NI S G N

6. Supervise the hiring, training, assigning, and evaluating of student assistants in Media Services.

   U NI S G N

7. Make recommendations for space utilization in the Media Center and television studio.

   U NI S G N

8. Make recommendations regarding equipment and supply needs for Media Services.

   U NI S G N

9. Formulate policies and procedures for the operation of the Media Center; develop and prepare handbooks, procedural and operational manuals, forms and letters.

   U NI S G N

10. Prepare statistical and narrative reports as necessary.

   U NI S G N

Legend: U = Unsatisfactory   NI = Needs Improvement   S = Satisfactory
         G = Good   N = Noteworthy

COORDINATOR OF MEDIA SERVICES
PAGE TWO

11. Review, select and recommend materials which will improve the library media collection.

U NI S G N

12. Plan, implement, and supervise the design and distribution of printed and other media relating to the operation and services of the Media Center.

U NI S G N

13. Plan, schedule, coordinate, and conduct programs, activities and tours of the Media Center.

U NI S G N

14. Serve as Media Services liaison with and consultant to G.C. personnel and the community.

U NI S G N

15. Develop and recommend goals and objectives for Media Services

U NI S G N

16. Assist in the development of overall goals and plans for the library.

U NI S G N

17. Assist in the development of the Media Services budget.

U NI S G N

18. Serve as library liaison with designated departments.

U NI S G N

19. Perform other library/media related duties and activities as assigned.

U NI S G N

20. Participate as a member of the faculty.

U NI S G N

Legend: U = Unsatisfactory   NI = Needs Improvement   S = Satisfactory
G = Good   N = Noteworthy

45

EMPLOYEE's COPY

COORDINATOR OF MEDIA SERVICES

	U	NI	S	G	N

	U	NI	S	G	N

	U	NI	S	G	N

	U	NI	S	G	N

	U	NI	S	G	N

Comments:

Review the job description and make any revisions necessary to reflect changes
in duties listed.

Outline any problems you have encountered in carrying out your job responsibilities.

List job-related priorities you wish to accomplish next year.

Signature of Evaluator   Dat

Super visor's Copy

COORDINATOR OF MEDIA SERVICES
PAGE THREE

	U	NI	S	G	N

	U	NI	S	G	N

	U	NI	S	G	N

	U	NI	S	G	N

	U	NI	S	G	N

Comments:

Review the job description and make any revisions necessary to reflect changes
in duties listed.

_____   _____
Signature of Evaluator   Date

PROFESSIONAL PERFORMANCE EFFECTIVENESS

JOB PERFORMANCE

Performs duties
in assigned position.
(Based on job
description)

Unsatisfactory	Needs Improvement	Satisfactory	Good	Noteworthy

Describe:

JOB KNOWLEDGE.

Possesses knowledge
in area of speciali-
zation.

Unsatisfactory	Needs Improvement	Satisfactory	Good	Noteworthy

Describe:

THOROUGHNESS

Follows through in
completing assignments.

Unsatisfactory	Needs Improvement	Satisfactory	Good	Noteworthy

Describe:

INITIATIVE

Meets or responds to
needs beyond area of
specialization.

Unsatisfactory	Needs Improvement	Satisfactory	Good	Noteworthy

Describe:

COMMUNICATION SKILLS

Communicates effectively
with colleagues, super-
visors and library users.

Unsatisfactory	Needs Improvement	Satisfactory	Good	Noteworthy

Describe:

SUMMARY   Georgia College

LIBRARY FACULTY EVALUATION

TO BE COMPLETED BY LIBRARY FACULTY AND SUPERVISOR

1. Discuss any changes to the employee's job description and prepare a mutually agreeable document that accurately reflects the job.

2. List any job-related problems that either of you have discovered and describe potential solutions.

3. List mutually agreeable job-related priorities for next year.

4. Review Part 3 of last year's performance evaluation. How effective were the solutions to problems listed on that form?

5. Review Part 3 of last year's performance evaluation. Which job-related goals were achieved? Which were not (indicate why not)?

I have read and discussed all   sections of this evaluation form.

_____

Supervisor   Title   Date

_____

Employee   Title   Date

_____

DIRECTOR OF LIBRARIES   Date

49

GEORGIA COLLEGE

January 1, 19 __ to December 31, 19 __

SUMMATIVE* EVALUATION OF FACULTY PERFORMANCE OF _____

	UNSATISFACTORY	NEEDS IMPROVEMENT	SATISFACTORY	GOOD	NOTEWORTHY

I. PROFESSIONAL PERFORMANCE EFFECTIVENESS

	UN	NI	SA	GO	NC
A. Possesses knowledge in area of specialization.					
B. Performs duties in assigned position.					
C. Follows through in completing assignments.					
D. Meets or responds to needs beyond area of specialization.					
E. Communicates effectively with colleagues, supervisors and library users.					

I. ACADEMIC ACHIEVEMENT/PROFESSIONAL DEVELOPMENT

	UN	NI	SA	GO	NC
A. Acquires knowledge and skills in area of specialization.					
B. Contributes knowledge to area of specialization.					
C. Serves area of specialization. (promotes service in)					

III. SERVICES TO INSTITUTION

	UN	NI	SA	GO	NC
A. Contributes to department goals.					
B. Serves on school/college committees					
C. Performs other college duties					

IV. PUBLIC SERVICE

	UN	NI	SA	GO	NC

ALL OF THE ABOVE JUDGEMENTS MUST BE DOCUMENTED WITH SUPPORTIVE EVIDENCE INCLUDED WI
THIS FORM. MATERIALS FROM INDIVIDUAL ANNUAL REPORTS ARE SUGGESTED. NOT VALID UNLE
SIGNED BELOW AND FACULTY MEMBER HAS INITIALED EACH PAGE.

_____ _____   _____ ___
Dept. Chairperson Signature   Date   Faculty Signature   Date
       (rater)   (person rated)

*Summative Evaluation is designed primarily for administrative evaluation of facul

II'DIVIDUAL FACULTY REPORT, 19___ Calendar Year

NAME _____

DATE COMPLETED _____

Please summarize the appropriate activities in which you have been involved since January 1, 19___, on the form below. Submit this information to the chairperson of your department by January 15, 19___ (the following year). This information will be used by your department chairperson, Dean, and Vice President for Academic Affairs to evaluate your performance for purposes of tenure, promotion, salary, and retention. This report covering faculty performance is based on the previous calendar year only. (Please print or type and read the form before completing.)

1. **Service to the College**

    a. Courses taught during this calendar year: 19___

	Winter Quarter	Spring Quarter	Summer Quarter	Fall Quarter
(1)				
(2)				
(3)				
(4)				

    b. Committee responsibilities, offices held:

       (1) Departmental

       (2) School.

       (3) College

    c. Other service (program coordinator, adviser to student organizations, etc.):

51

d.   Average number of student advisees during year:

2.   **Articles or Books Submitted or Published** (give complete citation, including co-authors)

3.   **Presentations at Professional Meetings** (give date, title and organization)

4.   **Book Reviews**

5.   **Editorships**

6. **Participation in Professional Associations, Workshops**

Membership	Conf/Meetings Attended	Date	Participation in Program	Offices Held/ Committees

7. **Grants or Proposals Submitted or Approved** (including Faculty Research Grants)

8. **Service to the Community**

   Membership in Organizations   Offices Held
   _____   _____

   Other Services

9. **Continuing Education Work**

   Program Development/
   Coordination/Instruction   Location   Enrollment
   _____   _____   _____

10. **Academic Work or New Degrees Earned**

    a.   Academic work (graduate and other)

    b.   New degree(s) received (college, date, title of degree)

11. **Other Activities of a Significant Nature** (Not Reported Above)
(i.e., recitals, public performances, exhibitions, clock-hours taught,
internships supervised, independent studies supervised, theses directed,
etc.)

12. **Department Chairperson's Evaluation** (to be shared with faculty member
before forwarding to Dean):

Georgia College

12. **Department Chairperson's Evaluation** (continued)

_____
Faculty Signature   Date

_____
Dept. Chairperson Signature   Date

(I have seen the above evaluation and I have been counseled by my department chairperson as required by Faculty Evaluation System.)

13. **Dean's Comments** (to be completed by Dean for each faculty member before forwarding to Vice President for Academic Affairs):

_____
Dean's Signature   Date

_____

COMMONWEALTH OF VIRGINIA

PERFORMANCE PLANNING AND EVALUATION

STRICTLY CONFIDENTIAL

Employee Name (Last, First, Middle)		Social Security Number
Position Number	Class Title	
Agency Code/Name		Sub-division
Performance Standards Due Date	Performance Evaluation Effective Date	

☐ Check here if this is a re-evaluation resulting from a score below 20.

An Equal Opportunity Employer

COMMONWEALTH OF VIRGINIA -- PERFORMANCE PLANNING

A. JOB ELEMENTS	B. WEIGHTS	C. PROFICIENT PERFORMANCE STANDARDS
Key words to describe the major elements of this employee's job.	A total of 10 weighting points indicating relative importance of the job elements. The more important elements have higher points.	A statement of the acceptable level of performance. Include quantity, quality and timeliness measures where possible. A maximum of eight and a minimum of three standards should be developed.
1.		
2.		
3.		
4.		
5.		
6.		
7.		
8.	TOTAL MUST EQUAL 10	

Changes during the performance year -- Must be initialed by employee, supervisor and reviewer.

DATE OF CHANGE _____

SIGNATURES INDICATE THAT THE CONTENTS OF THIS PLAN HAVE BEEN REVIEWED, AND IT IS UNDERSTOOD THAT THESE ARE THE PERFORMANCE STANDARDS FOR EVALUATING THIS EMPLOYEE.

EMPLOYEE 'S NAME		SIGNATURE	SOCIAL SECURITY NUMBER	DATE
SUPERVISOR'S NAME		SIGNATURE	SOCIAL SECURITY NUMBER	DATE
REVIEWER'S NAME		SIGNATURE	SOCIAL SECURITY NUMBER	DATE

Christopher Newport College

COMMONWEALTH OF VIRGINIA -- PERFORMANCE EVALUATION

D. EXTERNAL FACTORS Identify factors that directly affected the performance of each element	E. PERFORMANCE RATINGS For each standard written in Column C rate the employee's actual performance by circling the appropriate number. See definitions at the bottom of the page.	F. DOCUMENTATION For each rating of 0, 1 or 5 provide a descriptive explanation of actual performance of the job element that caused this rating to be given.
	0 1 2 3 4 5	
	0 1 2 3 4 5	
	0 1 2 3 4 5	
	0 1 2 3 4 5	
	0 1 2 3 4 5	
	0 1 2 3 4 5	
	0 1 2 3 4 5	
	0 1 2 3 4 5	

5 - Extraordinary performance as compared to the standard
4 - Substantially exceeded the proficient standard
3 - Somewhat exceeded the proficient standard
2 - Performed at the proficient standard
1 - Performed somewhat below the proficient standard
0 - Completely failed to perform the proficient standard

Attach additional pages if needed

COMMONWEALTH OF VIRGINIA -- PERFORMANCE EVALUATION

G. SCORES	H. SUPERVISOR'S (EVALUATOR'S) COMMENTS
For each standard multiply the weight in Column B across with the rating in Column E. Place the new value here.	Record here only those additional significant items which are not recorded elsewhere in this document.
1.	Indicate recommendations for further development and training.
2.	
3.	EVALUATED BY _____ PRINT NAME _____ SIGNATURE　　　　SOCIAL SECURITY NO.　　DATE
4.	I. REVIEWER'S COMMENTS
5.	
6.	
7.	REVIEWED BY _____ PRINT NAME _____ SIGNATURE　　　　SOCIAL SECURITY NO.　　DATE
8.	J. EMPLOYEE'S REVIEW Optional comments concerning the performance plan or evaluation for example, agreement or disagreement. I have reviewed this document and discussed the contents with my supervisor. My signature means I have been advised of my performance status and DOES NOT NECESSARILY IMPLY THAT I AGREE WITH THIS EVALUATION.
TOTAL SCORE Add down this column, G, for the total score and write this total on the line below.	_____ SIGNATURE　　　　SOCIAL SECURITY NO.　　DATE

EXTERNAL FACTORS WORKSHEET

K. EXTERNAL FACTORS

Consider external factors that may affect performance on these standards. Examples of external factors are staffing, equipment or supplies, budgetary needs, etc. For each job element, the supervisor and employee should identify external factors and actions to be taken to address the external factors for assisting the employee in meeting or exceeding the standard. List these factors and actions in the spaces provided below.

1.

2.

3.

4.

5.

6.

7.

8.

Form No. 129-   -040
Rev. 3/87

WESTMONT
A Christian College of Arts and Sciences

PERFORMANCE APPRAISAL
Administrative/Professional

Name _____   Position _____

Department _____   Supervisor _____

Hire Date _____ Time in Position _____ years _____ months

Date This Appraisal _____ Date Last Appraisal _____ Appraisal Period _____

APPRAISAL FACTORS
(Check one rating in each category)

O	Outstanding	**FM**	Fully Meets Requirements	**M**	Marginal
ER	Exceeds Requirements	**I**	Improving	**U**	Unacceptable

1.	**PRIMARY RESPONSIBILITIES** Consider degree to which position description responsibilities are accomplished.	Provide detailed comments and examples O ☐ ER ☐ FM ☐ I ☐ M ☐ U ☐
2.	**PLANNING/THINKING** Consider effectiveness in analyzing situations, proposing solutions, developing goals and standards, establishing procedures, forecasting and budgeting.	Provide detailed comments and examples O ☐ ER ☐ FM ☐ I ☐ M ☐ U ☐
3.	**ORGANIZING/EXECUTING** Consider effectiveness in assigning, communicating and accepting responsibility, authority, and accountability.	Provide detailed comments and examples O ☐ ER ☐ FM ☐ I ☐ M ☐ U ☐
4.	**LEADING/DIRECTING** Consider effectiveness in making decisions, selecting people, training and developing people, stimulating and energizing people, setting an example, and communicating with all levels of employees.	Provide detailed comments and examples O ☐ ER ☐ FM ☐ I ☐ M ☐ U ☐

			Provide detailed comments and examples
5.	**CONTROLLING/REGULATING** Consider effectiveness in adhering to standards and policies, measuring results, evaluating results, correcting results.	O ☐ ER ☐ FM ☐ I ☐ M ☐ U ☐	

OVERALL RATING

Assess overall performance based on weighing the importance of each appraisal factor to the particular job being appraised. (Check only one rating.)

☐ **OUTSTANDING** — Overall results **far exceed** expectations in **all major areas** of responsibility.

☐ **EXCEEDS REQUIREMENTS** — Overall results **consistently exceed** expectations in **most major areas** of responsibility.

☐ **FULLY MEETS REQUIREMENTS** — Overall results **consistently meet expectations** in **all major areas** of responsibility. May occasionally exceed expectations in some areas.

☐ **IMPROVING** — Overall results are **significantly better** but do not fully meet expectations yet. It is believed that a rating of "Fully Meets Requirements" is attainable. This rating may also apply to performance that has decreased to a level below "Fully Meets Requirements."

☐ **MARGINAL** — Overall results **erratic and/or frequently below expectations.** Improvement must be shown **and maintained** or the rating will become "Unacceptable."

☐ **UNACCEPTABLE** — Overall results **consistently below expectations.** Improvement must be shown within a designated period or termination will occur.

PERSONAL DEVELOPMENT PLAN

List those areas which you believe the employee must focus on to improve performance to an acceptable level.

AREA	ACTION PLAN	DATE RESULTS EXPECTED
1.		
2.		

OBJECTIVES

Assess last year's performance for each objective.

List those projects and/or programs that are high priorities next year. You may also include areas identified as challeng increase performance to an above standard level.

LAST YEAR _____	NEXT YEAR _____
Summarize results achieved for each objective established for this appraisal period.	State the objectives agreed to for the next appraisal period.

1. State the objective:

☐ Exceeded ☐ Achieved ☐ Partially Achieved ☐ Failed to Achieve

1. State the objective and how it will be measured:

2. State the objective:

☐ Exceeded ☐ Achieved ☐ Partially Achieved ☐ Failed to Achieve

2. State the objective and how it will be measured:

3. State the objective:

☐ Exceeded ☐ Achieved ☐ Partially Achieved ☐ Failed to Achieve

3. State the objective and how it will be measured:

4. State the objective:

☐ Exceeded ☐ Achieved ☐ Partially Achieved ☐ Failed to Achieve

4. State the objective and how it will be measured:

5. State the objective:

☐ Exceeded ☐ Achieved ☐ Partially Achieved ☐ Failed to Achieve

5. State the objective and how it will be measured:

OTHER COMMENTS

'se this space to specify and evaluate any other factors you feel are significant to properly and totally appraise performance.

EMPLOYEE COMMENTS (optional)

'he employee may use this space to handwrite any comments regarding this performance appraisal.

Appraiser's signature _____ Date _____

Reviewed by appraiser's supervisor _____ Date _____

Employee's signature _____ Date _____

The employee's signature verifies that this appraisal was given and does not necessarily indicate that the employee agrees with the appraisal.

(3/87)

 **Armstrong State College**

ANNUAL FACULTY EVALUATION

Professor's Name _____

Professor's Rank _____

Department _____

Evaluation Period from _____ to _____

To the Professor:

This evaluation will be filed in your official record and you will be given a copy. You may provide a written response to be filed with this evaluation. You have access to your official record upon request.

I acknowledge that I am aware of the contents of this evaluation.

Professor's signature _____ Date _____

To the Department Head:

Please attach to this form your evaluation of the professor whose name appears on the front of the form. This evaluation should be based on the information contained in the attached reports, must be in narrative form, and should cover teaching performance, scholarship, and service. If the performance is rated either "outstanding" or "unsatisfactory," this narrative should clearly indicate such. Moreover, in evaluating teaching performance, the department head should address whatever categories of teaching performance are appropriate to the professor's discipline.

_____ Date copy provided to professor.

Evaluator's signature _____ Date _____

Evaluator's name _____ Title _____

Effective Date 9/83

ARTICLE II.   EVALUATION AND PERSONNEL POLICIES

SECTION A.   Faculty Evaluation

The evaluation process serves multiple purposes.   It assists the college in its review of faculty members for continued employment; it assists the college in recognizing the merit reflected by the awarding of tenure and promotions; it helps in the determination of salaries; and it both recognizes and encourages a faculty member's professional growth.

The system presently in use at the college involves three successive evaluation levels.   On the first level, data is gathered from students, from peers, and from the individual faculty member.   This information is then included in the second level by department heads in making the official, annual evaluation of each faculty member's performance for a given academic year.   This official evaluation is recorded on the Annual Faculty Evaluation form that the department head completes for each department member.   Summaries of all data collected at the primary level are attached to it, and other appropriate information may be included.   These annual evaluations are then used at a third level of evaluation, where decisions are made regarding continued employment, tenure, promotion, and salary recommendations.

In March, 1975, the Faculty of Armstrong State College established an Evaluation Committee as a standing committee of the Faculty.   The duties of that committee as defined in the "Bylaws" are as follows:

> Evaluation Committee - The committee shall make recommendations to the Faculty concerning evaluation policies and procedures, including development, administration, and analysis of the evaluation system. It shall give technical assistance when requested in the assessment of the job performance of the Faculty and administrative officers assessed and to those officials responsible for the evaluation process of the college.   The membership shall consist of eight faculty members, two of whom shall be academic department heads.

SECTION A.1. Criteria for Faculty Evaluation

SECTION A.1.a. Teaching

Teaching effectiveness will be the most important single factor in all evaluations. Teaching includes all work that involves the use of a faculty member's expertise to communicate a subject matter to students. It may, therefore, include traditional lecturing in the classroom, supervision and training in a laboratory or clinical setting, nontraditional communication of a discipline, the collecting and developing of subject materials for communication to students, the guidance of students in independent study and research, and academic advising. A faculty member's command of the subject matter, motivation of and relationship to students, testing and upgrading practices, and overall fulfillment of teaching responsibilities are primary characteristics to be considered in the evaluation of teaching.

SECTION A.1.b. Scholarship

Scholarship involves the use of a faculty member's expertise as a scholar or artist. It includes work that adds to the subject matter of a discipline and work that increases the expertise of a faculty member as a professional. Research and publication are encouraged by the college; the pursuit and support of scholarly activities, consistent with the role of the institution, are professional obligations of every faculty member.

SECTION A.1.c. Service

Service includes all work that involves the use of a faculty member's academic status or professional expertise to benefit the college, the community or the profession. The essential element of service is that it involves contributions associated with a faculty member's established status in a discipline and at the college. Unless otherwise stipulated in a faculty member's job description, service is considered a responsibility of employment and consequently subject to evaluation.

SECTION A.1.d. Summary

Although the evaluation criteria indicated above point to three separate areas of evaluation, it is natural that the boundaries dividing teaching, scholarship, service, and other significant areas of professional activity may blur and that integrated enterprises involving these activities may emerge. The evaluation of the performance of a faculty member must, under any circumstances, be supported by appropriate corroborating evidence.

SECTION A.2. Procedures for Faculty Evaluation

SECTION A.2.a. The Annual Professional Activities Report (APAR)

The APAR instrument is distributed in September to each faculty
member. This report, covering the activities of an entire
calendar year (January-December), is completed by the faculty
member and submitted directly to the department head at the end
of the reporting period. A copy of this report must be attached
as an appendix to the Annual Faculty Evaluation of the faculty
member.

SECTION A.2.b. The Student Appraisal of Instruction and Course (SAIC)

The SAIC is administered at the college each quarter according to
the guidelines published by the Faculty Evaluation Committee and
approved by the faculty. Data from the SAIC are reported to the
department head and to the faculty member and must be included in
the Annual Faculty Evaluation report. A typed, verbatim
transcript of all Student Comment Sheets that are signed by
students will be given to the faculty member and to the
department head. If the Student Comment Sheet is unsigned, it
will be given only to the faculty member. Numbers and
percentages of responses on all categories of the SAIC are
aggregated annually on each faculty member according to lower
division, upper division, and graduate courses. The data will be
made available to the appropriate department head and dean and
may be used only for diagnostic purposes.

SECTION A.2.c. Faculty Peer Evaluation (FPE)

Each department has developed a peer evaluation system. A
summary of the record of performance of a faculty member in
teaching, scholarship, and service must be available for review
by peers prior to conducting a peer evaluation. The peer
evaluations need not be conducted annually and no faculty member
is required to evaluate any other faculty member. However,
designated peer evaluations must be conducted as follows:

1. Peer evaluations, with the faculty of a department participating, must be conducted at least twice for purposes of retention on nontenured faculty members. A third peer evaluation will normally be required at the time of a recommendation of tenure. The years designated for such peer evaluations should be scheduled at the time of the initial faculty appointment and any anticipated exceptions recorded at that time.

2. A peer evaluation involving all faculty of a department must be conducted at least one month prior to any recommendation for tenure or promotion.

3. Peer evaluations involving all faculty of a department must be conducted for all tenured faculty members during at least every five year interval after the award of tenure, in addition to any peer evaluation for promotion.

Designated peer evaluations must indicate the number of faculty colleagues in a department who support, do not support, or abstain from participating in the review of the record of the peer. Such results shall be reported in the retention, tenure, or promotion recommendation forms or in the Annual Faculty Evaluation form of the faculty member under review. All written comments solicited in a peer evaluation also shall be included in the official record. All peer evaluations conducted in addition to those designated above shall be reported in the Annual Faculty Evaluation form of the faculty member under review.

SECTION A.2.d. Annual Faculty Evaluation (AFE)

Each winter quarter, department heads evaluate the previous
calendar year's (January-December) professional performance of
faculty members on an Annual Faculty Evaluation form. The AFE
must address the foregoing criteria and standards for faculty
evaluations. Judgments rendered on the AFE are reached after
consulting the evaluatee's Annual Professional Activities Report
(APAR), Student Appraisal of Instruction and Course (SAIC),
Faculty Peer Evaluation report, if applicable, and such other
data collected during the preceding academic year as may be
deemed appropriate. Copies of pertinent reports must be appended
to the completed AFE instrument. The contents of the AFE must be
reviewed with the faculty member by the department head in a
scheduled conference. The faculty member receives a copy of the
AFE and signs a statement acknowledging awareness of its
contents.

The department head presents the AFE of each of the members of
the departmental faculty to the dean of the appropriate school.
The dean of the school and the department head discuss each
evaluation before transmitting it to the Vice President and Dean
of Faculty. The completed AFE instrument (with all appendices)
becomes a part of the faculty member's official record at the
college. Each faculty member has the right to insert into the
official record a written response to the AFE. When this right
is exercised, the faculty member's response becomes an appendix
to the AFE to which it pertains, and this appendix remains a part
of the AFE thereafter. The department head will acknowledge in
writing receipt of any response, noting changes, if any, in the
AFE made as a result of either the conference or the faculty
member's written response. This acknowledgement will also become
a part of the record. Grievances may be pursued through the
college's established grievance procedure.

SECTION A.3. Guidelines for Faculty Evaluation

The following guidelines indicate the types of specific information that are used to evaluate a faculty member's teaching, scholarship, and service.

SECTION A.3.a. Teaching

1. Each faculty member's Annual Professional Activities Report (APAR) contains a list of all courses taught during the year, as well as an appropriate description of all other teaching and teacher-related activities. This document must be appended to the faculty member's Annual Faculty Evaluation (AFE).

2. Data gathered from the SAIC must be included in the AFE report for each faculty member.

3. The supervision of independent study courses, laboratory or clinical learning experiences, and student research should be reported on a faculty member's APAR, and appraisals of these activities may be appended to the AFE.

4. The presentation of continuing education courses, seminars, or workshops should be reported on a faculty member's APAR, and appraisals of these activities may be appended to the AFE.

5. Appraisals by alumni may, where appropriate, be appended to the AFE.

6. Participation in the development of experimental and innovative instructional methodologies should be reported on a faculty member's APAR, and appraisals of this activity may be appended to the AFE.

7. Activities involving the counseling and advising of students should be reported on the faculty member's APAR, and appraisals of such activities may be appended to the AFE.

8. Appraisals of a faculty member's performance made during classroom visits by the department head or designated professional colleague(s) may be appended to the AFE.

9. In rendering an evaluation of teaching, both the number and nature of new course preparations by the faculty member and the number of freshman, sophomore, junior, senior, graduate and remedial level courses ought to be considered. This information should be reported on the APAR.

10. Any other factors which are considered important and which can be documented should be reported on the APAR, and documentation may be appended to the AFE. For example, faculty members have the responsibility to meet classes regularly and promptly and to make full use of the time scheduled for each class. They have the further responsibility to make themselves available to their students for academic advising. A faculty member's performance in meeting these basic responsibilities should be considered in completing the AFE.

SECTION A.3.b. Scholarship

1. Each faculty member's Annual Professional Activities Report (APAR) includes an appropriate description of all scholarly activities or areas of professional growth. This document must be appended to the faculty member's Annual Faculty Evaluation (AFE).

2. A Faculty Peer Evaluation completed for a faculty member must be attached to the subsequent AFE form.

3. Published scholarly papers and books, papers, and books in manuscript, and papers presented at meetings of learned societies or professional meetings should be reported on the APAR; appraisals or reviews thereof may be submitted as evidence of their scholarly value, and appended to the AFE.

4. Such activities as chairing sessions, serving as a panelist, or offering critiques at meetings of learned societies and professional organizations should be reported on the faculty member's APAR.

5. Participation in learned societies and professional organizations as an officer or a consultant should be reported on the faculty member's APAR.

6. Performances, exhibitions, or recitals should be reported on the faculty member's APAR and accounts or appraisals thereof may be submitted as evidence of their artistic value and as appendices for the faculty member's APAR.

7. Postdoctoral education and continuing graduate education leading to an advanced degree should be reported on the faculty member's APAR.

8. Grant proposals and their status as to funding or non-funding should be reported on the APAR and may be submitted as evidence of academic activity and as appendices for the faculty member's AFE.

9. Participation in, or support of, departmental seminars should be reported on the APAR.

10. Other creative expression related to a faculty member's profession ought to be reported on the APAR; accounts or appraisals thereof may be submitted as evidence of its scholarly or artistic value and as appendices for the faculty member's AFE.

SECTION A.3.c. Service

1. Each faculty member's Annual Professional Activities Report
    (APAR) will include an appropriate description of all
    service activities engaged in during the evaluation period
    in question. A copy of the faculty member's completed APAR
    will be appended to the Annual Faculty Evaluation Form
    (AFE).

2. An AFE must include as an appendix any Faculty Peer
    Evaluation conducted during the year under review.

3. Service to the profession can be demonstrated in a variety
    of ways. Such service often arises through membership in
    local, regional, national, or international professional
    organizations. Consequently, faculty members will report
    annually on the APAR their active memberships in appropriate
    professional organizations. Activities with professional
    organizations are to be reported on the APAR.

4. Service to the community may vary in importance from school
    to school and from department to department. Each
    administrative head should communicate clearly to each
    faculty member of the unit the importance of community
    service in the evaluation process. Evidence of service to
    the community may include, but need not be limited to,
    service to public agencies, professional consultation,
    public speeches reflecting the discipline and profession of
    a faculty member or reflecting the results of scholarship,
    cultural or artistic contributions and involvement and
    participation in civic organizations, charitable projects,
    and community service.

5. Service to the college may include, but is not limited to,
    contributions to special departmental, school, or college
    projects; working with students or faculty on
    extracurricular activities; active membership on department,
    school, or college committees; and participation in the
    public service, continuing education, or recruitment
    programs of the college. Such activities are to be reported
    on the APAR.

SECTION B. Evaluation of Administrators

A faculty committee has developed an instrument of evaluation of
the work of department heads, deans, Vice President and Dean of
Faculty, and the President.   Each faculty member is encouraged to
participate fully in the evaluation, which is a measurement of
performance, not of person.

Librarian_____   Date_____

This brief questionnaire is designed to enable the librarians working in the
Reference Room to help you better. These evaluations may also be used as
one of the criteria for promotion and tenure decisions.

For each statement listed below, circle the number which most accurately reflects your judgment about the librarian who worked with you on a specific
research or reference question.

    4. No improvement is needed (generally very good or excellent)
    3. Little improvement is needed (generally good performance)
    2. Improvement is needed (generally mediocre performance)
    1. Considerable improvement is needed (generally poor performance)
    NA Not applicable to this research or reference question

The librarian who worked with you:

4 3 2 1 NA   1. explained the use of reference books, indexes, and/or the
                  card catalog clearly and adequately.

4 3 2 1 NA   2. was interested in your reference question or in your research
                  needs.

4 3 2 1 NA   3. respected you and your ideas.

4 3 2 1 NA   4. was approachable and courteous.

4 3 2 1 NA   5. helped you understand more clearly your question or topic
                  of research.

Comments:

Please deposit the completed questionnaire in the box provided at the
Circulation Desk.

                Thank you.

Linfield College

STUDENT APPRAISAL OF LIBRARY INSTRUCTION

Course name_____   Date_____

Librarian_____

This brief questionnaire is designed to enable the librarians teaching in
your courses to improve their instruction. These evaluations may also be
used as one of the criteria for promotion and tenure decisions.

For each statement listed below, circle the number which most accurately
reflects your judgment about the librarian who provided instruction for this
class.

    4. No improvement is needed (generally very good or excellent)
    3. Little improvement is needed (generally good performance)
    2. Improvement is needed (generally mediocre performance)
    1. Considerable improvement is needed (generally poor performance)
    NA Not applicable to this class.

The librarian:

4 3 2 1 NA 1. knew the subject matter and was well prepared.

4 3 2 1 NA 2. presented information which was useful and relevant to the
             course.

4 3 2 1 NA 3. taught the class effectively.

4 3 2 1 NA 4. increased your knowledge of the library.

4 3 2 1 NA 5. encouraged discussion and answered questions satisfactorily.

Comments on the librarian's instruction:

STUDENT APPRAISAL OF LIBRARY INSTRUCTION
IN EFFECTIVE WRITING

Librarian_____   Date_____

This brief questionnaire is designed to enable the librarians teaching the
library week to evaluate their instruction. These evaluations may also be
used as one of the criteria for promotion and tenure decisions.

For each statement listed below, circle the number which most accurately
reflects your judgment about the library instruction you received in this
course.

   4. No improvement is needed (generally very good or excellent)
   3. Little improvement is needed (generally good performance)
   2. Improvement is needed (generally mediocre performance)
   1. Considerable improvement is needed (generally poor performance)
   NA Not applicable to this class.

The librarian:

4 3 2 1 NA   1. provided a clear outline of the library week.

4 3 2 1 NA   2. met with the class regularly and punctually.

4 3 2 1 NA   3. assigned useful and stimulating exercises.

4 3 2 1 NA   4. showed enthusiasm for the material and aroused interest.

4 3 2 1 NA   5. explained difficult material sufficiently.

4 3 2 1 NA   6. made clear the criteria by which students were evaluated.

4 3 2 1 NA   7. was available to students in the library.

4 3 2 1 NA   8. encouraged students to seek his/her help when necessary.

Comments on the library instruction week in Effective Writing:

Linfield College

FACULTY SELF-APPRAISAL

PROFESSIONAL EFFECTIVENESS, PROFESSIONAL DEVELOPMENT, SERVICE TO LINFIELD

A. GENERAL INFORMATION (All questions pertain to the most recent contract year)

Name_____ Date_____

Department of Appointment_____ Academic Discipline_____

Date of Appointment at Linfield_____ Total Years of Service to Linfield_____

Earned Degrees   Institutions   Year Ended

_____

_____

_____

Present Faculty Rank_____ Date of Appointment to Present Rank_____

Years in Rank_____ Tenure Status_____ Date Advanced to Rank_____

B. PROFESSIONAL EFFECTIVENESS

Evaluation of professional effectiveness for a faculty librarian is based upon a detailed position description and a statement of annual goals and objectives. Each year the librarian and the department head meet to review the position description and to establish goals for the coming year. Attach a current position description and statement of goals for the past year.

1. Comment on your professional performance during the past year. Include specific statements, as appropriate within the confines of your position description, on the following:

   A. The quality of your professional work at Linfield: organizational and managerial effectiveness, creativity, leadership, expertise, and other attributes as appropriate.

   B. Your relationship to the Linfield community: students, faculty, staff and others as appropriate.

2. Describe special accomplishments or projects of the past year which you feel contribute to the library's service to the college community. Include the general nature of projects, amount of time spent, goals, and results.

C. PROFESSIONAL DEVELOPMENT

1. Complete the following information for the preceding twelve months:

    a. Memberships in professional societies.

    b. Professional meetings attended (list organizations, places, and
        dates).

    c. Formal graduate studies completed at other institutions (list insti-
        tutions, courses, and dates).

    d. Continuing education seminars and workshops (list institutions or
        places, courses, and dates).

2. Describe and evaluate your contributions to the professional community
    outside the Linfield community:

    a. Service on committees, boards, etc. List the nature of the work
        and positions held.

    b. Research/publication projects. For each project, give the title and
        explain the nature of the project, goals, results, and significance
        to Linfield and the larger academic community.

D. SERVICE TO LINFIELD

Describe your involvement in faculty governance (committee assignments, for
example) and other contributions to the life and work of the college.

E. REVIEW BY DEPARTMENT HEAD

F. SIGNATURES

Faculty member_____Date_____

Department Head_____Date_____

Vice-President_____Date_____

COLLEAGUE APPRAISAL

A detailed position description and a statement of goals for the past year should be used as a basis for the evaluation of the professional effectiveness of a faculty librarian. Review these two documents and confer with the librarian you are evaluating before completing an evaluation.

Comment on the librarian's professional effectiveness, professional development and service to Linfield. You may wish to make specific reference to the following:

A. The quality of the librarian's professional work at Linfield.

B. The librarian's relationship tó the Linfield community: students, faculty, and staff as appropriate.

C. The librarian's contributions to the larger academic community.

Please include any additional comments which will aid the evaluation process.

UTICA COLLEGE

REFERENCE LIBRARIAN--PERFORMANCE EVALUATION

Name_____   Date _____

Title_____

Period Covered by this Review _____

Reason for Review _____

Choice of : A. Always performs at this level; B. Usually performs at this level.
or C. Performance Needs improvement.

REFERENCE INTERVIEW STANDARDS

1. Conveys an attitude and manner that encourages users to seek assistance. A B C
   Comments:_____
   _____

2. Attempts to ascertain level of knowledge/sophistication of patron.
   Provides assistance at the appropriate level of need.
   Comments: _____
   _____

3. When assigned desk duty, always maintains a profile of high visibility.
   Comments: _____
   _____

4. Acknowledges patrons waiting for assistance. Alert to patrons needing
   help, but not asking for it.
   Comments: _____
   _____

KNOWLEDGE OF RESOURCES

1. Demonstrates a thorough knowledge of basic reference tools.
   Comments: _____
   _____

2. Demonstrates knowledge of general collection, card catalog and resources
   of other departments in the library.
   Comments: _____
   _____

PERFORMANCE EVALUATION (continued)   Choice of:
                                                        A B C

3. Demonstrates subject knowledge, within his/her own area of responsibility
    as liaison with division/dept. of college. _____

    _____

SEARCH STRATEGY

1. Determines the real question, by interviewing the patron and suggesting
    alternate approaches the patron might use to satisfy his/her information
    needs. _____

    _____

2. Provides needed instruction in use of sources to both patron in need of
    information, and to the student assistant he/she may be supervising.

    _____

    _____

3. Able to plan and execute effective search strategies for complex or ex-
    tended reference questions. _____

    _____

OVERALL PERFORMANCE

    _____
    _____
    _____
    _____

EMPLOYEE'S COMMENTS

    _____
    _____
    _____

Employee Signature:_____ Date:_____
Reviewed by: _____ Date: _____

KENTUCKY STATE UNIVERSITY
Library Faculty Self-Evaluation Form

ame _____ Date _____

itle and Academic Rank _____

ear Colleague:

ne means of up-grading professional effectiveness is self-evaluation. To facilitate
he process I have devised the attached questionnaire, which I am asking you to fill
ut. Completing the questionnaire will be useful in two ways: First and foremost,
t will get you to think about your own strengths and shortcomings. (You probably
valuate your own work continually, but the questionnaire should help you to do it in
more formal, perhaps more precise, way.) Second, it should add a dimension to my
nderstanding and appreciation of you as a librarian.

would ask that you try to avoid two common pitfalls in your self-appraisal: First,
o not let modesty keep you from being very explicit about your assets. Second, try
o be equally candid about your shortcomings. As librarians and as students of
articular disciplines we are well aware that individuals are less knowledgeable in
ome areas of a discipline than in others, just as they have both good days and bad
ays at work. We also appreciate only too well that every librarian has certain
ethods and approaches with which he is very comfortable and adept, as well as those
ith which he is less proficient.

Sincerely,

D. W. Lyons
Director of Libraries

WL:ffg

aculty Questionnaire

Section I - General Information

. Within library science, which area or areas do you regard as your strongest?

85

2. Which area do you regard as your weakest?

3. What is your greatest asset as a librarian?

4. What is your greatest shortcoming as a librarian?

5. Describe what you have found to be most gratifying in your work at Kentucky State University.

6. Describe what you have found most disappointing or frustrating in your work at Kentucky State University.

7. Describe your present duties and responsibilities.

8. Are there areas of your job in which you feel you need additional experience and training? If so, please describe and explain your plan for meeting those needs.

9. What aspects of your job interest you the most?

0. What aspects of your job interest you the least?

1. Are there changes which you would like to see made in your job so that you could improve your performance? If so, how would these changes benefit the library services unit?

Section II - Professional Experience

1. Start with the current year and list the types of experience by year/years that you
    have had subsequent to receiving your undergraduate degree.

2. For hom many years, including this year, have you been employed at K. S. U.?

Section III - Professional Involvement

1. List those professional organizations in which you participate:

    a. as a member
    b. as an officer (please list the office held)

2. List professional conferences and workshops attended during the past year.

3. List papers, seminars, workshops or exhibits you have presented during the past yea

    Please list dates and places of presentation.

Kentucky State University

4. List any proposals you have written for the University during the past year:

    a. Place an asterisk beside those proposals funded.
    b. Place two (2) asterisks beside those proposals presently being reviewed by a funding agency.
    c. List those proposals for which you were a contributing writer.

5. List any research project in which you are involved. Describe your role in these research projects.

6. List any papers, articles or essays published during the past year:

7. If you feel that the above list does not fully reflect your professional activities during the past year, please submit a statement indicating those activities which, in your opinion, should be included in evaluating your academic performance in the area of professional involvement.

Section IV - University Service

1. List the University and departmental committees on which you serve.

    a. For each committee on which you serve, please designate whether you were elected (E), appointed (A), or volunteered (V).

    b. Have you regularly attended and actively participated on all of these committees? If not, please state your reasons.

    c. Place an asterisk beside any committees on which you acted as the chairperson.

2. List the activities that you have participated in which promote either the University or the library (i.e. clinics, workshops, institutes, recruiting efforts, speakers' bureau, etc.)

3. List the activities or involvements that you have had with student organizations (i.e. sponsor, advisor, homecoming, social groups, fraternities, sororities, etc.)

Section V - Supplementary Information

1. List the earned degrees that you hold and the institution from which they were received.

2. What honors have you received?

3. Have you undertaken advanced graduate studies subsequent to receiving your M.S.L.S.?

4. If your answer to number three was yes, please list the names of the courses that you have taken and the number of credits received for each course.

5. Have you been admitted to a Specialist, Advanced Certificate, or Doctoral program? If so, list the name of the institution and the discipline.

6. Have you ever thought about leaving the field of librarianship for another discipline?

7. Do you think that transferring to another area within the library services unit would increase your effectiveness?_____If your answer is yes, specify the area.

8. List the public school teaching, librarian, or administrative certificates that you hold.

9. If you are employed in the library services unit next fiscal year, list the personal work objectives that you intend to accomplish during the ensuing year.

. List the titles of the professional journals that you read on a regular basis.

. List the titles of five of the most recent books that you have read.

. During the past year, I have attended the following number of faculty meetings:

        A. None _____

        B. A Few _____

        C. Most _____

        D. All _____

. Are you a member of the American Association of University Professors?

. Describe the efforts that you have made to recruit students to attend Kentucky State University. (Be sure to tell how many potential students that you contacted.)

. Of the potential students that you contacted, how many enrolled?

93

**SUPPORT STAFF PERFORMANCE
APPRAISAL DOCUMENTS**

PERFORMANCE APPRAISAL GUIDELINES   Williams College

<u>General Instructions to the Supervisor</u>: Carefully evaluate employee performance in each
area indicated. Be certain you consider each factor separately and on the basis of the
performance for the preceding year (for example, because a person was habitually tardy,
that person should not necessarily be penalized on the quality of work, although a
problem with tardiness could explain quantity). If you wish you may place a check mark
by the statement that most accurately assesses employee performance under each general
area, although space for comments under each job performance area has been provided
should the suggested performance guidelines not meet your needs. For those general areas
not pertinent to the performance evaluation, mark N/A (not applicable). At the end of
the evaluation form a larger area has been provided for more general comments or for an
overall summary of your evaluation.

EMPLOYEE NAME: JOB TITLE:

DEPARTMENT:

<u>Dependability</u>: Degree of supervision needed to carry out job duties or assignments to
completion.

____ Rarely needs supervision on routine work; may only need general guidance in
new assignments or special projects.
____ Very dependable on routine aspects of work; may require some specific
guidance on projects or work which occurs infrequently or on new assignments.
____ May need guidance in routine aspects of work, with more direct supervision on
new assignments.
____ May need more frequent guidance in routine work, with assistance provided in
prioritizing work and job methods.

Comments:

<u>Adaptability</u>: Ability to learn quickly; ability to adjust to changes in job assignments,
methods, office equipment, personnel or surroundings.

____ Very quick to catch on, showing initiative in new assignments or changes in
job methods or office equipment.
____ Is accepting of change and shows flexibility in learning new assignments,
methods or equipment.
____ May tend to resist changes, and as such, seems reluctant or hesitant in
learning new methods or equipment.
____ Has difficulty adapting to changes and is resistant to learning new methods
or equipment.

Comments:

Williams College

Attendance: Consideration of number of absences, times arriving tardy, length of lunch
periods, number and length of coffee breaks.

____ Consistently on time, rarely misses work, very punctual.
____ May be occasionally late or absent but well within normal limits.
____ May be missing work, arriving late more than he or she should.
____ Has problems in missing work, punctuality or misuse of breaks.

Comments:

Cooperation: Willingness to take supervision from one or more than one supervisor,
recognizing the value of establishing objectives or priorities; ability to
get along with co-workers.

____ Responds very well, showing great initiative in own work and helping other
employees as well.
____ Is responsive to supervision and works well with co-workers.
____ May have some reluctance in accepting guidance from more than one supervisor
or has some problems with co-workers.
____ May be resentful of guidance and efforts of co-workers.

Comments:

Quantity of Work: Ability to meet or surpass assigned workload; consider use of time
during the regularly scheduled workday and frequency of use of
overtime.

____ Rarely misses deadlines and may often be ahead of schedule.
____ Makes good use of workday and produces assigned work on time.
____ May have "peaks and valleys", occasionally falling behind in work and may
require overtime to catch-up.
____ Is having difficulty keeping up, requiring frequent overtime or help in
completing assignments.

Comments:

Quality of Work: Consideration of accuracy, and attention to detail of work; ability to organize; need to re-do work.

_____ Exceptionally accurate, with constant attention to detail; very organized.
_____ Usually is both thorough and attentive; few errors are made and the need to re-do work infrequent; well organized.
_____ Work is acceptable but needs to be more attentive to detail and accuracy; may have to re-do work more frequently than he or she should.
_____ Accuracy is a problem and needs to be more attentive to detail.

Comments:

Job Knowledge: Degree of familiarity with job procedures and equipment essential to the job; ability to be innovative.

_____ Has completely mastered all phases of job, showing initiative in adapting equipment, systems and procedures as needed.
_____ Has a thorough knowledge of most phases of work, and handles procedures and equipment with competence.
_____ May need to develop more thorough knowledge of some phases of the job in order to effectively use equipment, systems and procedures.
_____ Has problems in proper use of equipment or application of systems and procedures; may be relying on other workers or supervisor for guidance.

Comments:

Interpersonal Relations: Ability to communicate effectively with co-workers, members of the College community and general public; the degree to which positive image is conveyed and sustained.

_____ Communicates very effectively by being consistently courteous and responsive to any inquiry or need.
_____ Is usually positive and supportive in contacts with the College community and general public.
_____ May at times seem impersonal or somewhat perfunctory in dealings with the general public or College community.
_____ May be brusque and does not always convey a positive image.

Comments:

98

ADDITIONAL COMMENTS:

My supervisor has reviewed and discussed his/her evaluation of my job performance.

_____   _____
Employee signature   date

To the supervisor: Please sign and return the completed form to the Personnel Office.

_____   _____
Supervisor signature   date

WESTMONT
A Christian College of Arts and Sciences

PERFORMANCE APPRAISAL
Staff

Name _____   Position _____

Department _____   Supervisor _____

Hire Date _____ Time in Position _____ years _____ months

Date This Appraisal _____ Date Last Appraisal _____ Appraisal Period _____

APPRAISAL FACTORS
(Check one rating in each category)

---

1. **QUANTITY**

   Consider ability to meet or surpass goals, frequency of need for extra hours and use of time during normal workday.

   - ☐ Almost always exceeds goals.
   - ☐ Always meets and sometimes exceeds goals.
   - ☐ Meets goals the great majority of the time. Consistent results.
   - ☐ Misses goals too often and/or inconsistent productivity.
   - ☐ Rarely meets goals. Requires constant help to complete work.

   Provide detailed comments and examples

---

2. **QUALITY**

   Consider accuracy, attention to detail, neatness, need to re-do work, and organization of work.

   - ☐ Errors are rare. Exceptional neatness and attention to detail.
   - ☐ Very few errors and typically minor. Very neat.
   - ☐ Acceptable number of errors. Good organization of work.
   - ☐ Too many errors. Requires improved accuracy and/or neatness.
   - ☐ Accuracy poor. Frequent re-work.

   Provide detailed comments and examples

---

3. **DEPENDABILITY**

   Consider degree of supervision needed to carry out tasks to completion to meet job requirements.

   - ☐ Needs minimal supervision. Usually self-starts.
   - ☐ Needs little supervision. Often self-starts.
   - ☐ Needs normal supervision. Sometimes self-starts.
   - ☐ Needs frequent supervision.
   - ☐ Needs constant supervision.

   Provide detailed comments and examples

ADAPTABILITY

Consider ability to learn quickly, and to adjust to changes in job assignment, methods, people or surroundings.

- ☐ Extremely fast learner. Welcomes new assignments. Undisturbed by change.
- ☐ Learns quickly. Adjusts well to change.
- ☐ Learns well. Usually accepts change.
- ☐ Learns with difficulty. Resists change.
- ☐ Does not grasp or is forgetful of assignments. Fights change.

Provide detailed comments and examples

INTERPERSONAL RELATIONS

Consider willingness to accept supervision, cooperate with co-workers, accept goals and objectives, communicate effectively, and project positive image.

- ☐ Exceptional support of the department. Often performs beyond requirements. Projects outstanding image.
- ☐ Always positive, courteous, professional. Projects above average image.
- ☐ Usually positive, supportive, courteous. Projects good image.
- ☐ Impersonal and/or uncooperative at times. Lacks professionalism.
- ☐ Negative attitude. Does not communicate well. Conveys poor image of the organization.

Provide detailed comments and examples

ATTENDANCE

Consider number of absences, lateness, length of meal and break periods.

- ☐ Rarely absent or late, adheres to schedules.
- ☐ Infrequently absent or late, adheres to schedules.
- ☐ Occasionally absent, usually on time, adheres to schedules.
- ☐ Inconsistent attendance, punctuality, adherence to schedules.
- ☐ Serious number of absences, lateness, abuse of work schedules.

Provide detailed comments and examples

LEADING OTHERS

Consider effectiveness in completing work assignments through others, and training others.

- ☐ Frequently exceeds desired output of a work group. An excellent trainer. Sets an outstanding example.
- ☐ Usually produces and sometimes exceeds desired output of a work group. A very good trainer.
- ☐ Usually produces desired output of a work group. A good trainer.
- ☐ Frequent difficulty in controlling a work group's output. A marginal trainer.
- ☐ Has great difficulty controlling a work group. A poor trainer.

Provide detailed comments and examples

Westmont

OVERALL RATING

Assess overall performance based on weighing the importance of each appraisal factor to the particular job being appraised.
(Check only one rating.)

☐ **OUTSTANDING** — Overall results **far exceed** expectations in **all major areas** of responsibility.

☐ **EXCEEDS REQUIREMENTS** — Overall results **consistently exceed** expectations in **most major areas** of responsibility.

☐ **FULLY MEETS REQUIREMENTS** — Overall results **consistently meet expectations** in **all major areas** of responsibility. May occasionally exceed expectations in some areas.

☐ **IMPROVING** — Overall results are **significantly better** but do not fully meet expectations yet. It is believed that a rat of "Fully Meets Requirements" is attainable. This rating may also apply to performance that has decreased to a level below "Fully Meets Requirements."

☐ **MARGINAL** — Overall results **erratic and/or frequently below expectations.** Improvement must be shown **and maintained** or the rating will become "Unacceptable."

☐ **UNACCEPTABLE** — Overall results **consistently below expectations.** Improvement must be shown within a designated period or termination will occur.

PERFORMANCE/DEVELOPMENT OBJECTIVES

List those areas which you believe the employee must focus on to either improve performance to an acceptable level, or to challenge performance to above standard level.

AREA	ACTION PLAN	DATE RESULTS EXPECTED	PURPOSE
1.			☐ Raise to Stand ☐ Challenge Bey Standard
2.			☐ Raise to Stand ☐ Challenge Bey Standard

OTHER COMMENTS

Use this space to specify and evaluate any other factors you feel are significant to properly and totally appraise performance.

EMPLOYEE COMMENTS (optional)

The employee may use this space to handwrite any comments regarding this performance appraisal.

Appraiser's signature _____ Date _____

Reviewed by appraiser's supervisor _____ Date _____

Employee's signature _____ Date _____

The employee's signature verifies that this appraisal was given and does not necessarily indicate that the employee agrees with the appraisal.

PERFORMANCE EVALUATION 1987–1988

The evaluation form has been created after consultation with both employees and supervisors. It is likely that the form and the format of the evaluation process will be further modified in the future to reflect the experiences and observations of both employees and supervisors. No single form will ideally meet the precise requirements of each individual job, employee and supervisor. Supervisors may make minor changes in the form or process to accommodate this reality. Any questions with reference to the form or process may be directed to the Director of Personnel.

I.   Instructions

The Personnel Office will distribute forms to each department.

A.   Step One, Section I

Normally the employee will complete Section I, but in those instances where a supervisor oversees a number of employees with the same job title and responsibilities, the supervisor may rank the major responsibilities at his/her discretion.

B.   The supervisor will review Section I as completed by the employee and make the appropriate comments in Sections II and III.

C.   The key to the ratings to be employed in the evaluation process is at the bottom of page 1 and at the top of page 2.

D.   The supervisor will complete Section IV, but evaluate the employee only on those traits which are applicable to the position.

E.   The supervisor will complete Section V and then review the evaluation with his/her department head.

F.   The supervisor and/or the department head will review the evaluation with the employee. The employee may make additional comments in Section V or add comments on a separate sheet of paper to be attached to the evaluation.

G.   The department head will review the evaluations with his/her principal administrator and then return the completed forms to the Personnel Office.

PERFORMANCE EVALUATION 1987–1988

IAVERFORD

Name _____ Job Title _____

Time period: From _____ To _____ 19 _____

I. EMPLOYEE LIST OF MAJOR RESPONSIBILITIES, IN ORDER OF PRIORITY		II. REVIEWER PRIORITY ORDER AND RATING, PLUS COMMENTS		
ority	Responsibility	Priority	Rating	Comments

III. REVIEWER MAY ADD ADDITIONAL RESPONSIBILITIES EXPECTATIONS AND COMMENTS

Responsibility	Priority	Rating	Comments

KEY TO RATINGS: 5 = Outstanding   4 = Above average   3 = Satisfactory   2 = Needs improvement   1 = Not satisfactory

IV. PERFORMANCE EVALUATION	Outstanding	Above average	Satisfactory	Needs improvement	Not satisfactory	Not applicab
OVERALL JOB KNOWLEDGE Knowledge of requirements, methods, techniques and skills in doing the job	☐	☐	☐	☐	☐	☐
Comments _____						
QUALITY OF WORK Caliber of work produced or accomplished	☐	☐	☐	☐	☐	☐
Comments _____						
TIME MANAGEMENT Ability to use time constructively	☐	☐	☐	☐	☐	☐
Comments _____						
INITIATIVE Extent to which employee is a self-starter in attaining objective of the job	☐	☐	☐	☐	☐	☐
Ability to work with minimum supervision	☐	☐	☐	☐	☐	☐
Comments _____						
DEPENDABILITY Reliability in assuming and carrying out commitments, obligations and assignments	☐	☐	☐	☐	☐	☐
Comments _____						
JOB ATTITUDE Amount of interest and enthusiasm shown in work	☐	☐	☐	☐	☐	☐
Comments _____						
PLANNING AND ORGANIZATION Ability to plan and organize workload to meet normal and unexpected priorities	☐	☐	☐	☐	☐	☐
Comments _____						
SECURITY SENSITIVITY Ability to handle confidential information	☐	☐	☐	☐	☐	☐
Comments _____						
INTERPERSONAL SKILLS Ability to interact effectively with supervisor	☐	☐	☐	☐	☐	☐
Ability to interact effectively with others (peers, clients, etc.)	☐	☐	☐	☐	☐	☐
Comments _____						
ATTENDANCE AND PUNCTUALITY Attendance	☐	☐	☐	☐	☐	☐
Punctuality	☐	☐	☐	☐	☐	☐
Comments _____						

V. OVERALL EVALUATION

    ☐ Outstanding   ☐ Above average   ☐ Satisfactory   ☐ Needs improvement   ☐ Unsatisfactory

Comments _____

_____

_____

_____

_____

_____

Evaluator's signature _____ Date _____

Department Head's approval (if applicable) _____ Date _____

Performance discussion with employee   Date _____

Employee's comments _____

_____

_____

_____

_____

_____

Employee's signature _____ Date _____

    Your signature indicates that this report has been discussed with you

Performance Evaluation for Library/Media Staff   Georgia Co

Employee's Name _____   Date _____

Social Security No. _____   Reason for Report: Check Appropriate Category

Department _____

☐ Annual Report   ☐ End of Probationary Period

☐ Termination   ☐ Transfer or Special

Instructions: Prepare evaluation in accordance with the guidelines regarding performance evaluations for
classified employees of   College. Rating terms are as follows.

RATING TERMS:

Outstanding - Truly exceptional performance generally attained by no more than an exceptionally small
number of an organization's employees.

Exceeds Requirements - Superior performance that surpasses what is generally expected of employees a
majority of the time.

Meets Requirements - Competent day-to-day performance is attained. Any shortcomings are generally
balanced by some superior performance characteristics. This level of performance is generally attained by the
majority of an organization's employees.

Needs Improvement - Day-to-day performance generally shows some limitations that are not balanced by any
superior performance characteristics. This level of performance is generally demonstrated by only a small
number of an organization's employees.

Unsatisfactory - Day-to-day performance shows significant limitations and definite need for improvement is
noted. This level of performance is generally demonstrated by no more than an exceptionally small number of an
organization's employees.

I. WORK SKILLS

A.   Quality of Work.   Consider thoroughness and accuracy in job performance.

1. ☐ Unsatisfactory	2. ☐ Needs Improvement	3. ☐ Meets Requirements	4. ☐ Exceeds Requirements	5. ☐ Outstanding

B.   Quantity of Work.   Consider amount and timeliness of work completed.

1. ☐ Unsatisfactory	2. ☐ Needs Improvement	3. ☐ Meets Requirements	4. ☐ Exceeds Requirements	5. ☐ Outstanding

C.   Adaptability.   Consider flexibility and ability to adjust to changing procedures and
requirements.

1. ☐ Unsatisfactory	2. ☐ Needs Improvement	3. ☐ Meets Requirements	4. ☐ Exceeds Requirements	5. ☐ Outstanding

D.   Initiative and Creativity.   Consider innovativeness, originality, suggestions, attempts
to improve work, and ability to implement ideas in the work place.

1. ☐ Unsatisfactory	2. ☐ Needs Improvement	3. ☐ Meets Requirements	4. ☐ Exceeds Requirements	5. ☐ Outstanding

Category Evaluation: 4-6 ☐ Unsatisfactory   14-17 ☐ Exceeds Requirements
                             7-9 ☐ Needs Improvement   18-20 ☐ Outstanding
                            10-13 ☐ Meets Requirements

108

II. LEARNING SKILLS

A. Aptitude for Learning. Consider the ability to grasp essentials, ideas, procedures, and techniques.

1. ☐ Unsatisfactory	2. ☐ Needs Improvement	3. ☐ Meets Requirements	4. ☐ Exceeds Requirements	5. ☐ Outstanding

B. Professional Development. Consider participation in professional organizations, workshops, coursework, and other activities that enhance one's job performance.

1. ☐ Unsatisfactory	2. ☐ Needs Improvement	3. ☐ Meets Requirements	4. ☐ Exceeds Requirements	5. ☐ Outstanding

C. Job Knowledge. Consider proficiency in use of procedures, materials and equipment required for job completion and the ability to work independently.

1. ☐ Unsatisfactory	2. ☐ Needs Improvement	3. ☐ Meets Requirements	4. ☐ Exceeds Requirements	5. ☐ Outstanding

Category Evaluation:
- 3-4 ☐ Unsatisfactory
- 5-7 ☐ Needs Improvement
- 8-10 ☐ Meets Requirements
- 11-13 ☐ Exceeds Requirements
- 14-15 ☐ Outstanding

III. INTERPERSONAL SKILLS

A. Cooperation and Attitude Toward Work. Consider enthusiasm and general disposition.

1. ☐ Unsatisfactory	2. ☐ Needs Improvement	3. ☐ Meets Requirements	4. ☐ Exceeds Requirements	5. ☐ Outstanding

B. Dependability.. Consider responsible work habits, consistency of performance, reliability, punctuality, and work attendance.

1. ☐ Unsatisfactory	2. ☐ Needs Improvement	3. ☐ Meets Requirements	4. ☐ Exceeds Requirements	5. ☐ Outstanding

C. Interpersonal Relationships. Consider the ability to work effectively and tactfully with patrons, colleagues, and supervisors.

1. ☐ Unsatisfactory	2. ☐ Needs Improvement	3. ☐ Meets Requirements	4. ☐ Exceeds Requirements	5. ☐ Outstanding

D. Communication Skills. Consider the ability to write, speak, and listen effectively to others.

1. ☐ Unsatisfactory	2. ☐ Needs Improvement	3. ☐ Meets Requirements	4. ☐ Exceeds Requirements	5. ☐ Outstanding

E. Approachability. Consider openness, receptiveness, and availability.

1. ☐ Unsatisfactory	2. ☐ Needs Improvement	3. ☐ Meets Requirements	4. ☐ Exceeds Requirements	5. ☐ Outstanding

Category Evaluation:
- 5-7 ☐ Unsatisfactory
- 8-11 ☐ Needs Improvement
- 12-16 ☐ Meets Requirements
- 17-21 ☐ Exceeds Requirements
- 22-25 ☐ Outstanding

IV. JOB SPECIFIC SKILLS

A. Job Description. Consider the employee's knowledge of assigned duties and the overall performance of all of the duties specified in the job description.

1. ☐ Unsatisfactory	2. ☐ Needs Improvement	3. ☐ Meets Requirements	4. ☐ Exceeds Requirements	5. ☐ Outstanding

Category Evaluation: 1 ☐ Unsatisfactory   4 ☐ Exceeds Requirements
2 ☐ Needs Improvement   5 ☐ Outstanding
3 ☐ Meets Requirements

V. OVERALL PERFORMANCE RATING

Consider all categories carefully, giving most weight to those factors more important in the job. After balancing strengths and weaknesses, rate the **overall** execution of duties as a composite appraisal of the employee's job performance.

☐ Unsatisfactory   ☐ Meets Requirements   ☐ Outstanding
☐ Needs Improvement   ☐ Exceeds Requirements

VI. COMMENTS AND SUGGESTIONS

To be completed by the supervisor.

VII.

If Probationary Report, recommended for continued employment?   ☐ Yes   ☐ No

If Termination Report, recommended for re-employment?   ☐ Yes   ☐ No
(If **no** applies to either of the above, explain the reason under Comments.)

Review period from _____ to _____
                                              Date   Date

** _____
                     Employee's Signature

_____
                     Supervisor's Signature

_____   _____   _____
                     Reviewer's Signature   Reviewer's Title   Date

** Employee's signature not required on a termination report.

VIII. JOB—RELATED GOALS FOR NEXT YEAR

The employee and the supervisor jointly establish some job-related goals to be accomplished during the next year. List them below.

PERFORMANCE APPRAISAL FORMAT

Section I provides several measures or standards of performance which are inherent to most jobs. Each employee is to be evaluated in the Series (A) categories of measurement. Series (B) relates to supervisory and administrative personnel.

PERFORMANCE STANDARDS

Exceeds Expectations: Significantly and consistently performs at level above that expected. Achieves results beyond most people at this level.

Meets Expectations: Meets major requirements; is consistently effective and competent. Achieves results expected from people at this level.

Meets Minimum Level Expectations: Needs improvement to be fully satisfactory. Fails to meet some requirements. Satisfactory results could be achieved through a reasonable amount of development or change.

Fails to Attain Expectations: Work is overall unsatisfactory. Improvement possibilities questionable.

WINTHROP COLLEGE

RECORD OF PERFORMANCE APPRAISAL

NAME _____ DEPT. _____ DATE _____

POSITION _____ REASON FOR EVALUATION _____

Series A - Check appropriate level of performance for each item.

1. **Quality of Work** - the extent to which the employee neatly, thoroughly, and accurately completes job assignments according to established standards of quality.

   ☐ Exceeds Expectations   Comments: _____
   ☐ Meets Expectations   _____
   ☐ Meets Minimum Level Expectations   _____
   ☐ Fails to Attain Expectations _____

2. **Quantity of Work** - the extent to which the employee produces an amount of acceptable work in order to meet schedules over which he or she control.

   ☐ Exceeds Expectations   Comments: _____
   ☐ Meets Expectations   _____
   ☐ Meets Minimum Level Expectations   _____
   ☐ Fails to Attain Expectations _____

3. **Knowledge of Job** - overall concept and knowledge of technical, administrative, and routine duties involved in the job. Competence in understanding and performing complex tasks.

   ☐ Exceeds Expectations   Comments: _____
   ☐ Meets Expectations   _____
   ☐ Meets Minimum Level Expectations   _____
   ☐ Fails to Attain Expectations _____

4. **Initiative** - the extent to which the employee recognizes or anticipates tasks to be performed and begins without waiting for instructions to do so.

   ☐ Exceeds Expectations   Comments: _____
   ☐ Meets Expectations   _____
   ☐ Meets Minimum Level Expectations   _____
   ☐ Fails to Attain Expectations _____

5. **Interpersonal Relations** - degree of cooperation and interaction with co-workers, supervisor, or other personnel, and the public. Demonstration of positive attitude toward job and college environment.

   ☐ Exceeds Expectations   Comments: _____
   ☐ Meets Expectations   _____
   ☐ Meets Minimum Level Expectations   _____
   ☐ Fails to Attain Expectations _____

I

6. **Dependability** - consider behavior under normal conditions as well as conditions of stress. Reliability in job performance and availability when needed are key factors in determining degree of dependability.

    ☐ Exceeds Expectations   Comments: _____
    ☐ Meets Expectations   _____
    ☐ Meets Minimum Level Expectations   _____
    ☐ Fails to Attain Expectations   _____

7. **Safety/Security** - awareness of dangerous conditions and/or practices and action to remedy such problems.

    ☐ Exceeds Expectations   Comments: _____
    ☐ Meets Expectations   _____
    ☐ Meets Minimum Level Expectations   _____
    ☐ Fails to Attain Expectations   _____

8. **Organization of Work** - planning and organizing of work assignment in a manner which minimizes time wasted and duplication of effort.

    ☐ Exceeds Expectations   Comments: _____
    ☐ Meets Expectations   _____
    ☐ Meets Minimum Level Expectations   _____
    ☐ Fails to Attain Expectations   _____

9. **Communications** - ability to communicate with others in job related functions, and properly instruct in area of speciality.

    ☐ Exceeds Expectations   Comments: _____
    ☐ Meets Expectations   _____
    ☐ Meets Minimum Level Expectations   _____
    ☐ Fails to Attain Expectations   _____

10. **Judgment** - demonstration of sound judgment by action taken during the course of performing duties. Consider ability to make decisions affecting corrective or normal operation procedures that have a positive result.

    ☐ Exceeds Expectations   Comments: _____
    ☐ Meets Expectations   _____
    ☐ Meets Minimum Level Expectations   _____
    ☐ Fails to Attain Expectations   _____

Series B - For Supervisory/Administrative Personnel

11. **Goal Accomplishment** - quality and quantity of accomplishment toward set goals, also consider responsiveness to organizational goals.

    ☐ Exceeds Expectations   Comments: _____
    ☐ Meets Expectations   _____
    ☐ Meets Minimum Level Expectations   _____
    ☐ Fails to Attain Expectations   _____

2

12. **Conceptualization and Flexibility in Problem Resolution** - ability to conceive potential problem situations and take positive action. Consider situations not normally part of routine job duties.

☐ Exceeds Expectations Comments: _____
☐ Meets Expectations _____
☐ Meets Minimum Level Expectations _____
☐ Fails to Attain Expectations _____

13. **Supervision/Leadership** - quality of leadership in obtaining employee cooperation and influencing employee behavior.

☐ Exceeds Expectations Comments: _____
☐ Meets Expectations _____
☐ Meets Minimum Level Expectations _____
☐ Fails to Attain Expectations _____

14. **Planning and Delegation** - ability to plan and coordinate activities, manage personal and employee time effectively, distribute work loads, and delegate responsibility and authority without loss of supervisory control.

☐ Exceeds Expectations Comments: _____
☐ Meets Expectations _____
☐ Meets Minimum Level Expectations _____
☐ Fails to Attain Expectations _____

15. **Employee Development** - provide guidance, counseling, and meaningful training and instruction in development of employee skills and potential.

☐ Exceeds Expectations Comments: _____
☐ Meets Expectations _____
☐ Meets Minimum Level Expectations _____
☐ Fails to Attain Expectations _____

16. **Evaluation** - demonstration of valid and consistent evaluations of subordinates. Also consider attitude, preparedness, and approach to employee evaluation.

☐ Exceeds Expectations Comments: _____
☐ Meets Expectations _____
☐ Meets Minimum Level Expectations _____
☐ Fails to Attain Expectations _____

17. **Commitment to Affirmative Action/Equal Employment Opportunity** - consider sensitivity to special problems of minority employees or students, willingness to assist career advancement of minority employees, receptiveness to hiring qualified minority applicants, and attention to the outlined hiring procedures.

☐ Exceeds Expectations Comments: _____
☐ Meets Expectations _____
☐ Meets Minimum Level Expectations _____
☐ Fails to Attain Expectations _____

3

EMPLOYEE DEVELOPMENT ANALYSIS

Section II should provide a basic analysis of employee status, needs, and current potential. The supervisor should specify development plan and the suggested time frame of accomplishment.

I. ELEMENTS OF PERFORMANCE

Major Strengths

_____

_____

_____

_____

Opportunities for Improvement

_____

_____

_____

_____

Plan of Individual Development (Specific)

_____

_____

_____

_____

II. SUMMARY OF EVALUATION

_____

_____

_____

_____

_____   _____
Rating Officer   *Employee*

_____
Reviewing Officer

The employee is requested to sign the performance evaluation with the understanding that such signature does not constitute approval or disapproval on the part of the employee.

116

WINTHROP COLLEGE

SUMMARY RATING REPORT

Name _____   Position Title _____

Unit or Dept. _____   Date _____

Based on a review of the above named employee's performance during the current review period, as recorded on the attached appraisal form, the summary rating for this rating period is:

☐   Exceeds Expectations

☐   Meets Expectations

☐   Unsatisfactory

_____
Rating Officer

_____
Reviewing Officer

Certification by Employee

By signing this form I am certifying only that the rating indicated above has been shown to me. The fact that I have signed this form should not be interpreted as either agreement or disagreement with the rating given.

_____   _____
Date   Employee

Staff Self-Evaluation Form

NAME: LAST   FIRST   M.I.   PERIOD COVERED

TITLE OF EMPLOYEE_____

Section I - Efficiency Report

Care and fairness to the employee and the Library should be exercised in completing this rating. Base your judgment on the entire period covered and not on isolated incidents.

Rating columns: OUT-STANDING | VERY GOOD | GOOD | ADEQUATE | INADEQUATE | NOT APPLICABLE | NO CHANCE TO OBSERVE

JOB PERFORMANCE

- Accuracy
- Adjustment to a large variety of tasks
- Alertness
- Consistency in checking for and correcting errors
- Ease of learning techniques and procedures
- Industry
- Initiative
- Neatness and orderliness of work
- Quantity of work output
- Self-control and courtesy in dealing with the public
- Thoroughness

PERFORMANCE UNDER SUPERVISION

- Ability to work without close supervision
- Acceptance and use of criticism
- Dependability in carrying out instructions
- Judgment and ability to make decisions
- Willingness to do work assigned

PERSONAL QUALITIES

- Consideration in requesting changes in schedules
- Dress and personal appearance
- Loyalty
- Physical vigor: Energy and endurance
- Punctuality
- Quality as a team worker
- Self-control & courtesy in dealing with library staff
- Sense of responsibility
- Separation of personal life from job
- Willingness to meet necessary changes in schedule
- Cooperates with administrators, supervisors, and fellow workers

ction II - General Information

Describe what you have found to be most gratifying in your work at Kentucky State University.

Describe what you have found most disappointing or frustrating in your work at Kentucky State University.

Describe your present duties and responsibilities.

Are there areas of your job in which you feel you need additional experience and training? If so, please describe and explain your plan for meeting those needs.

What aspects of your job interest you the most?

6. What aspects of your job interest you the least?

7. Are there changes which you would like to see made in your job so that you could improve your performance? If so, how would these changes benefit the library services unit?

Section III - Supplementary Information

1. List the earned degrees that you hold and the institution from which they were received.

2. List the certificates/diplomas that you earned from business/technical schools.

3. Do you think that transferring to another area within the library system would increase your effectiveness? _____ If your answer is yes, specify the area.

. If you are employed in the library services unit next fiscal year, list the personal work objectives that you intend to accomplish during the ensuing year.

. List the titles of five of the most recent books that you have read.

. Describe the efforts that you have made to recruit students to attend Kentucky State University. (Be sure to tell how many potential students that you contacted.)

. Of the potential students that you contacted, how many enrolled?

8. How many cultural/fine arts events that were presented on campus during the past year did you attend?

9. How many K. S. U. athletic events did you attend during the past year?

10. As an employee of Kentucky State University, I consider myself to fall into the following category:

        _____ An outstanding employee.
        _____ A very good employee.
        _____ A good (satisfactory) employee.
        _____ An adequate employee (sometimes fails to perform in a satisfactory manner).
        _____ An inadequate employee (definitely unsuited for the type of work that he/she is doing).

Signed _____

Date _____

DWL:12/1/78

122